The Golf Widow Travels -
Scotland

The Golf Widow Travels - Scotland

Getting your dream vacation
With or without
A golfer in tow

Karen Sanders Howe

Golf Widow Travels
Seattle, Washington

The Golf Widow Travels – Scotland

Getting Your Dream Vacation

With or Without

A Golfer In Tow

Requests for permission should be sent to the publisher:
Golf Widow Travels
13123 Palatine Ave. N.
Seattle, WA 98133
www.http://golfwidowtravels.com

Editor: Trisha Benson Davis
Cover Design: Christina Scott
http://home.earthlink.net/~xtinascott

Printed in the United States of America

ISBN: 0-9743822-0-5

Lovingly Dedicated To:

My Dad whose love of travel inspired me
My Mom for her adventurous spirit
Allen and Jan who supported every crazy scheme
Steve who challenged me to write
Trisha, college roommate and editor extraordinaire
And my cheering section, the 3Ms, Marilyn, Melissa
and Mercedes

MAP OF SCOTLAND

CONTENTS

Golf Widow - The Definition

Golf Widow \galf wido\ *n* (first invented in Scotland in the early 1700s but in common usage by 1927) a woman left alone, abandoned by the golfer bent on a 7:00 am tee time, a leisurely 18-holes on the course and a very long 19th in the clubhouse. The golfer is usually accompanied by one or more "widowmakers".

~1~

The Golf Widow's Plan

You don't have to be a "golf widow" to put this guide to use. You may have been deprived of the traveling companion of your dreams by football, fishing, model railroading or a successful career. Maybe you are mired down with an old stick-in-the-mud or, worse yet, your biological clock could be ticking. I don't mean your "baby clock," I mean the "I don't want the tour director pushing my butt and my walker up onto the Grannies Day Out Bus clock".

If you are a woman longing for travel beyond K-Mart and the Safeway parking lot, married or single, *The Golf Widow Travels – Scotland* will show you there is no need to wait for your self-directed partner or a phase of the moon to coincide with your best friend's bank account. Just stand in front of the mirror and say "I'm going to Scotland!" until you believe it.

You'll find this guide has divided Scotland into 10 distinct regions and each region has several golf courses around which the touring revolves. This is a ploy that can be used by true "Golf Widows" to get the old duffer on the plane with his clubs. Just get to Scotland by hook or by crook, I say! Let him think you are sacrificing for him.

The real reason for centering this guide around these regional golf courses is that, in general, golfers are nice, friendly people who like to stay in nice, friendly places while on their golf vacations. And aren't those the kind of people and places we want to be around when we travel alone? Scotland, the home of golf, has built a fine reputation on its hospitality based golf industry. This hospitality holds true whether you are staying in posh resort style hotels or budget bed and breakfasts. You'll have no worries about being in the wrong part of town, the wrong side of the tracks or waking up to a drunken traveling salesman at your door.

Traveling With A Golfer?

Why would you accompany a golfer to Scotland, even encourage and applaud the trip plan, when you know you've spent other golfing vacations pouting in the bar or having the wrong color rinse applied by yet another strange hairdresser?

You know "alone". You are a "golf widow," so get over it and use "alone" to your advantage. Use this guide as a marital aid or a recipe for a well spent holiday in the towns and villages of the Scottish countryside by getting your golfer on a course and "your" day underway.

Now here are five great reasons for suggesting a golf trip to Scotland:

1. How many more times do you want to fry yourself poolside in Palm Springs?

2. Think of the delight in your golfer's eyes when you say, "Honey, I'd love to see you play a round on the Old Course."

3. Castles, lilting melodies, shop doorbells, men in kilts, gorgeous fabrics woven before your eyes, Sean Connery and a "cuppa" tea with new friends.

4. After a day on your own, you walk refreshed, confident and mysterious into the lounge bar, straight over to the old duffer and reward him with a kiss that tells him 6 over par is a very respectable day.

Not with a golfer? Here is Number 5 but it could just be your Number 1.

5. How many more fun trips to the Mall of America or weekend stays at the Luscious Lady Spa with your four best friends can you endure?

Why Do I Travel "Alone"?

Friends and acquaintances ask this question along with "How can you do that?" and "You must be very brave?" I have never heard these utterances fall from their mouths if my trip is for work.

All over the country women kiss the kids and hubby good-bye, climb on a plane that will take them thousands of miles away for a conference or fact finding mission and no one questions them. But just let that businesswoman say "I'm going, alone, to San Francisco to see The Mark Morris Dance Company" and she might as well be going to the moon.

I want to go, and see, and do what's out there and this, more often than not, does not fit into friend's or relation's schedules. If I wait any longer for Prince Charming to whisk me off to Edinburgh, I won't be able to get up on his damn horse.

I love looking, touching, smelling, and tasting new things, and meeting very ordinary and very interesting people. At home, I'll take my cup of coffee to the end of the pier to see what that guy just dropped in his bucket. I'll talk to the kid walking the ferret and I'll blatantly gawk at a family, walking four abreast in a crowded shopping mall while eating drippy ice-cream. People amaze and amuse me. I'm curious.

When I travel in Scotland I do the same things but with the added twist of old and ancient landscapes and architecture as a backdrop. I don't know why but you put that ice-cream smeared family in front of their 400-year-old home and I am fascinated. How do they live? What color is the living room? What is the kitchen like? What is it like to go back and forth between centuries?

My imagination has always been very active and lying cozy in my Laura Ashley coordinated room with the en-suite bath, I wonder who lived under these eaves when they were dark and unheated.

I love looking in the windows of the greengrocer, butcher, baker and the chemist. They still sell traditional items along with the up-to-date. One of my favorite examples of this is Haggis, that much maligned but very adaptable Scottish meatloaf dressed as a sausage. It is still available in its original bulbous form or, as sold in Pitlochery, the ever trendy Haggis Lasagna. Now whip down to your corner market and try to find either one of those delicacies.

Art and Architecture are two of my main areas of interest and I am very fulfilled in Scotland. The architecture is art and vice-a-versa so I am doubly blessed, but it is often the totally unexpected that grabs my interest.

On my last trip I collapsed in front of the television with a case of jet lag. Being too tired to change the channel, I watched a special on racing pigeons. Racing pigeons? Once armed with this new information, I spotted pigeon cotes in back gardens, met a fellow who bred pigeons for racing, stopped alongside the road and watched as two young men hoisted large wicker cages out of a car, checked their watches, made their calculations and set birds to flight. The birds wheeled around and somehow headed for home. I pulled back onto the road with map in hand and promptly got lost.

An interest in a person's hobby can make you instantly something more than a stranger. The bird breeder was anxious to share his experience and cups of tea were poured, sandwiches shared (I always carry some biscuits or sweets so I can share too) and I found out as much about him as he did about me. You part friends and sometimes - lifelong friends. Don't worry about your time schedule when this kind of event happens - one stately home looks like another over time - but that funny man with a bird on his head will never be forgotten.

I may be alone at times, but I'm never lonely.

The Ticket To Travel -

Destination Scotland

Having chosen Scotland as your destination remember, if you are spending a week or ten days in Scotland you don't want to waste two of those precious days getting there. Try to fly directly into Prestwick, Glasgow, or Edinburgh. This may involve an airport transfer but you will be saving time.

When you look at the map and see London just down the road from Scotland, please don't think you'd like to just pop into downtown London to see the Queen. You'll have bags to deal with, at least a 30 to 45 minute train or bus ride into midtown, and then on top of all that you will be jet lagged and as stiff as a board. So take my suggestion and stay in the airport, have a drink to olde London town, and get on the next flight to Scotland.

Do Your Homework

You can armchair travel your whole life and wind up well traveled - from the chair to the bathroom, to the fridge, and on Monday morning... to work. My advice: get a map and start asking around about travel agents. Friends and complete strangers will offer up horror stories or the name of the "best" agent or mention their cousin, Betsy, who works at Where to Now? Travel. Take those names and then interview. This is your adventure and you don't want it screwed up by some bozo who "knows" Hawaii and Mexico. You need knowledge to be a savvy traveler.

Speaking of being a savvy traveler there is a great shop in Edmonds, Washington called The Savvy Traveler (425.744.6076). This little shop has everything from blow-up pillows and dual voltage appliances to specialty travel books and snazzy luggage. Your town or region may have a shop like this. Find it, browse the guides and pump the help for recommendations.

A superb place to get started with your research is The British Tourist Authority. They can be reached in the U.S. at 1.800.GO 2 BRITAIN or in Canada at

1.888.VISIT UK. Give them an idea of what you'd like on your trip agenda and a nice packet will arrive at your doorstep to get you jazzed.

The extensive series of guides put out by the Scottish Tourist Board is worth a look. They have guides specifically for bed and breakfasts, guesthouses or small hotels, and even self-catering small rental cottages and camping facilities. The complete range is available by mail from The Travel Shop, 551 Fifth Ave. Suite 702, New York, NY 10176 or by calling 212.490.6688. The Travel Shop is a division of The Rail Europe Group and right next door to the British Tourist Authority, so they are a font of information as well.

You can also contact the Scottish Tourist Board directly at 23 Ravelston Terrace, Edinburgh EH4 3TP. Their e-mail address is info@stb.gov.uk.

The following addresses are regional Scottish Tourist Board offices that correspond with the regions this book will be visiting. They can help with region specific questions and accomodation.

Regional Tourist Boards:

GALLOWAY AND DUMPHRIES – SOUTHWEST
64 Whitesands, Dumfries DG1 2RS, Ph. 138.725.3862, Fax 135.724.5555 or www.dumfries and galloway.co.uk

THE WEST - AYRSHIRE
Customer Information Centre, 15 Skye Road, Prestwick KA9 2TE, Ph. 129.267.8100, Fax 129.247.1832 or www.ayrshire-arran.com

GLASGOW
11 George Square, Glasgow G2 1DY, Ph. 141.204.4400, Fax 141.221.3524 or www.seeglasgow.com

HIGHLANDS & ISLANDS
Peffery House, Strathpeffer IV14 9HA, Ph. 199.742.1160, Fax 199.742.1168 or www.highlandfreedom.com

THE CENTRAL REGION
Lower City Mills, West Mill St. Perth, PH1 5QP, Ph. 173.862.7958, Fax 173.863.04416 or www.perthshire.co.uk

THE NORTH
Use the same addresses and numbers as the Highlands & Islands.

THE GRAMPIAN REGION
27 Albyn Place, Aberdeen AB10 1YL, Ph. 122.428.8828, Fax 122.458.6861 or www.castlesandwhisky.com

ST. ANDREWS AND THE KINGDOMS OF FIFE AND ANGUS

70 Market Street, St. Andrews KY16 9NU, Ph. 133.447.2021, Fax 133.447.8422 or www.standrews.com

EDINBURGH

Edinburgh & Scotland Information Centre, 3 Princes St. Edinburgh EH2 2QP, Ph. 131.473.3800, Fax 131.473.3881 or www.edinburgh.org

THE BORDERS

Shepard's Mill, Whinfield Road, Selkirk TD7 5DT, Ph.870.608.0404 or www.scot-borders.co.uk

Your local public television station can also be a source of information. Here in Seattle, every weekday evening Rick Steves (also of Edmonds) hosts *Europe Through the Backdoor*. These half-hour programs feature Rick's travel videos and his great ideas for economical and family friendly travel throughout Europe. Call 425.771.8303 for Rick's free newsletter or log on to www.ricksteves.com.

National Public Radio station is another great place to get background material. Call your local station for information about Rudy Maxa's *The Savvy Traveler* segment on *MARKETPLACE*. Watch for his public television series also.

In depth travel assistance may be as close at hand as your local community college or sporting goods store (REI here in Seattle has travel events). Just keep your eyes open.

The Grand Tour

A myriad of companies offer tours that can range from the 5-star historic inn with chauffeur to the simple bus and budget variety. There are even self-drive tours with prearranged hotels. I have tried them all at one time or another and given your tolerance level, pocket book, and adventurous spirit, they all have their place. Freedom of choice can be limited and sometimes you may feel like you are on a forced march. But you'll see more of Scotland on a tour than you would from your rocking chair in Dubuque.

If you must consider the needs of a golfer on your vacation, then you might want to contact a tour company that specializes in golf tours. They can be pricey but nothing is too good for your golfer and the gorgeous brochures will help in your travel planning. I've found the following companies to be very helpful: Wilkinson Golf and Leisure (1.800.868.1106) and InterGolf (1.800.468.0051).

The Internet

Cybertravel is a marvelous way to lose yourself for weeks at a time. My "Favorites" list has nice generic mega sites and funky little town sites.

The Scottish Tourist Board is a well-oiled machine that is constantly updating and preening its web site. They can help you find lodging, enter a contest, bake shortbread, and direct you to specialty tours. Their site address is www.holiday.scotland.net and a very good place to start planning.

I have only one word of caution about using the Internet for booking and confirming lodging. That word is "Caution". In the rush to get everyone up-to-date and on-line, e-mail services have been offered to establishments without direct access to computers. Mrs. MacWhozit's Bed and Breakfast in the Caringorms may depend on her weekly trip to the regional library for a look at e-mail. I really prefer the old fashioned mail when dealing with small establishments or the phone if you can deal with accents.

If any establishment, large or small, has a fax number listed this is far superior than mail and at the moment, the Internet. A fax puts the date, time of arrival, and length of stay right there on their desk in black and white without the wait for international mail service or the unexpected use of a delete key.

You can purchase your airline tickets on-line but do your homework before you do so. Check prices and the small print. Do you want to trust a large travel site like Expedia or Priceline, or go directly with your favorite airline to get more air miles?

Several trips ago I used Priceline and got caught up in the "bidding" mindset of naming my own price. I bid ridiculously low and didn't get a ticket, so I bid a little higher and didn't get the ticket. On my third try I got what I considered a deal on my ticket but I also felt like I was throwing darts at a wall of fares and dates. I think I would have felt better about the experience if I had been a little more prepared. So here is what I would now recommend:

1.   Know what kind of prices you can get from your regular airline choices. Call them and ask. Specify dates and destinations and get firm prices. Do not rely on the newspaper ads that tout really good prices but in actuality the price is only good on the second Thursday after a Blue Moon.

2.   Have your travel dates firmly in mind and a calendar in front of you in case you have to make changes.

3.   What departure and arrival times are convenient for you? Often good prices are available on less than convenient flights. Arriving in Glasgow at 4am could leave you snoozing on a park bench waiting for the rental car agency to open or your room to be vacated.

4.   How many layovers and plane changes can you tolerate to save a few dollars? A four hour layover in the Copenhagen Airport could be torture for many of us.

Whether you log onto the Internet, phone your airline or use a travel agent, the most important thing you can do is Get That Ticket!

Safety

The number one question I was asked while doing research was "Is it safe?" My answer is always the same - "As safe as staying home". This is not the most reassuring answer considering the muggings, children with guns, killer bees and roving bands of men on that anti-impotence drug and all of this within 2 blocks of home.

Once again let's come back to the businesswoman starting off on a trip. She does research on her hotel, has a recommendation from a friend, or she has a respected travel agent who knows her needs. If she is smart she is using all the resources at her command to make that trip safe and comfortable. It is just common sense she'd do the same thing when traveling for pleasure in a strange, new place.

Common sense is often better than a burly bodyguard. Think of the scuzziest street in your town. Think midnight. Think two drunks coming out of Benny's Bar. If you can actually think of yourself in this scenario then I hope it's their payday and you make a few bucks. I'll bet you can't imagine putting yourself in this predicament at home so why would you on vacation? If you want to frequent the local nightspots just remember the beer is stronger, the booze is drunk differently and all the men sound like Sean Connery.

A shipboard's romance, or in this case a Highland Fling, can be lots of fun, but be careful and prepared. Most towns do not have an all night drug store in case of an emergency romantic situation, so it's best to take your own intimate protection.

Remember that your mother always told you "don't talk to strangers." In this case don't talk to people who make you feel strange. Use your intuition and common sense, keep moving or politely excuse yourself to the ladies room (in the next building) if you are feeling uncomfortable.

If all else fails and you need help, ask for it. If you're lost, feeling ill, or just need some reassurance stop a lady on the street, go into a shop or pull up to a house with the laundry flapping in the breeze and ask for help. I've yet to be turned away.

If you find yourself in a truly dangerous situation, the police can be reached by dialing 999 on all telephones.

Money

Always a topic of interest for me, money has a way of flying out of my hands and always twice as fast when I'm on vacation. Having lived in Britain and traveled on business, I've tried all sorts of ways to carry and spend the damned stuff. Cash, traveler's checks, credit cards and even a checking account at a posh London bank have traveled with me fairly successfully. Some advantages or disadvantages to them are:

Cash

1.   Use the bank at your destination airport if you haven't gotten your hometown bank to supply you with a starter packet of British Pounds.

2.   Carry only what you need. Have a little more to get you through the weekend.

3.   Do not carry a huge wad of bills.

4.   Money belts are ugly, uncomfortable and stupid. So there! I might consider one if I were going to the continent where quick-fingered thieves are everywhere but in Scotland I carry my cash and passport with me in my shoulder strap purse. More hints about that purse later.

5.   Carry only enough good old U.S. dollars to get you through duty-free, the bar on the way to your destination and what you'll need to get home once you land in the good old U.S.A.

Travelers Checks

1.   Better than carrying large amounts of cash.

2.   Try to get British currency checks.

3.   The best exchange rate will be at a bank. Beware of Foreign Exchange kiosks without bank affiliation. The bank across the street will be a better bet.

4.   Not every shop will know the current exchange rate if your checks are in dollars.

5.   Some shops, accommodations and restaurants may not have enough cash to make change for you. You may want to consider small denomination checks.

Credit and Debit Cards

1.   My favorite!

2.   Make sure your credit limit is able to carry you through your stay! Talk to your banker. Sometimes they will raise your limit for a specified amount of time.

3.   If you are going with a debit card make sure you have enough to debit!

Checking Account

Too much trouble for just a vacation.

Warning!

I'd like to go back to my favorite way to deal with money - credit and debit cards and the ATM. Read this and heed my warning!

I entered the world of cyber-banking late in life. No big deal you say, but the millennium had almost arrived and I'd never touched an ATM. When I admitted to this oddity, my friends looked at me as if I still ironed my crinolines. But it was true and I admit it to you. I actually go into my bank during working hours and speak to a real person. I also have a grocery store that coddles this oddity and they take my check for just about any amount of cash. I'm not computerphobic. I just like the ambiance and the interaction with that living, breathing person.

So, in the mail came a debit card to my savings and checking account. I screwed up my courage and called the info number on the back of the card and admitted my sin to a lovely young woman who helped me see the error of my ways. 66,000 ATMs around Britain would accept my card and they were ready and waiting for me.

How did it work out? I guess I need to tell the tale and offer some pre-travel suggestions.

When I landed I was prepared to hit the road. Friends had met me at O'Hare for my three-hour layover and we drank some of my dollars, but there were still a few in my pocket, enough for the layover on the way back. I had about 40 pounds left over from a previous trip. I had my Visa credit card and that wonderful debit card that would magically deplete my savings account. I was set. I was confident. I got into my rental car and hit the road.

My first night I ate in my hotel, crashed and used my credit card in the morning. My first shock was at a village shop where I tried to use my pounds. No problem, right? Wrong! The bills I clutched had been recalled and a fancy new variety was now in use. I could change them in the bank on Monday. Monday! It was Sunday and I was in a village without a bank. Oh well.

We sorted out the bills and change and I was able to afford my picnic lunch.

In the next town, dinner was easy - just break out the old credit card. The bed and breakfast was easy ... I would scope out the surrounding streets for a bank with an ATM and get cash in the morning before I'd packed my bags. I slept peacefully.

In the morning I took out my Versatel debit card and stepped confidently up to the town's only ATM. My card had all the correct information on it - Visa, Versatel and the international Plus insignia. I inserted the card into the machine. I answered the questions and waited when told to wait for my cash. The notification that my card was declined was not a welcomed message. In fact, I tried again thinking I'd botched my code or missed some subtle computer thing. Declined! I got in line inside the bank and tried to remain calm while my card was scrutinized by a teller and the bank manager. They then handed the card back to me with the advice that I try another bank up the road in the larger town.

Being ever resourceful, I pulled out my antique pound notes. The bank manager squinted at them and exchanged them for new. I was rich again and could pay my landlord at the bed and breakfast. Now I was on a mission ... get money out of an ATM and soon!

In the town of Ayr, I had a long shopping precinct to walk and several different banks to choose from. I headed out. I met some very nice bank employees.

Doesn't sound good does it? When you use an ATM you are usually outside on the sidewalk not inside talking with the staff. I was inside because my card kept receiving the "sorry declined" message. At the fourth bank my card worked. I went inside and tried to find out the reason for this miracle. The manager wasn't sure but thought it had to do with which bank my card was affiliated. The 66,000 banks of the promotional material didn't seem to ring true. But I'd found <u>my</u> bank - The Bank of Scotland. I stuck with it.

<u>ASK</u> your banker <u>BEFORE</u> you go which banks will accept your card and don't take the promotional material as gospel. Make your banker work for you and make your trip a breeze, or have a nail biting adventure going from ATM to ATM with visions drifting through your head of living in a cardboard box on the streets of Ayr.

Ready, Set, Go!

All righty now! Let's go over our Pre-Trip Planning List.

The homework was to get the plan, a ticket, safety tips and money in your purse. I think we've got it covered.

Remember the very most important item is the ticket. Without a ticket you ain't goin' nowhere and what's the point of that?

I have always been known to say "All I need to have is the ticket". What I really mean is "All I need is my purse and a ticket". Since September 11, 2001, I have begun to carry my passport in my purse just because it seems easier to grab than trying to get my driver's license out of the wallet slot if someone asks for I.D.

Now we are armed with the essential trip items and information, so let's get on to some of my helpful hints and hideous horrors that may make your trip easier.

Oh Lord! I knew I'd forgotten something on my Planning List. I can't be too much at fault because I've never had one to worry about, but you just might have one - "The Golfer".

You'll have his bag packed with stacks of new polo shirts, his home course sweater, and crisp, conservative slacks, (make up some silly excuse about Jack and Arnie not wearing pastels this summer). You'll have polished his putter and spit-shined his shoes. Yee Gods, this sounds like you're traveling with a child! If this is the case then be sure to pin his name and address to his new windbreaker/raincheater and you're off.

~2~

Helpful Hints and Horror Solutions

I have been traveling alone for over 35 years. I made my first business trip to the British Isles when I was not more than 20 years old and each and every trip has been a learning experience. I've been smug about some travel triumphs and I've still not told a soul about some of the disasters. Trading tales of the most embarrassing events on my front porch is not an option.

What follows are some hints that may help in your travels. Hopefully you'll be able to laugh at some of my missteps and know that you could handle the same predicament with greater poise. I'm not a professional traveler, great white hunter, thrill seeker or intellectual. I just like traveling and I hope you can use my hints to your advantage.

Luggage - Aaagh!

I will be <u>painfully</u> honest with you. I hated my suitcase, even though I went out and got a lovely tapestry, "roll-a-round" case. I proudly wheeled that baby with all my reference books and sundry "neededs" into the airport and turned it over to the airline to be checked straight through. I wheeled that baby through customs and out to my rental car, popped it into the trunk and set off. I hated that suitcase. Why?

My first hotel had a flight of stairs and a fire door at the top, a hallway not much wider than the bag and two more fire doors before I finally muscled that beast into my room.

Why didn't Ross have the distinctive tapestry case in a medium size on display? The price was fabulous but... Were my eyes bigger than my back was strong? Why didn't I follow my own advice? I knew the Duchess was on Corfu and that extra posh frock was true folly on my part. There was no one to blame but myself (damn). I ended up cursing that thing at every lift – up or out. Sure I looked terrific wheeling along on the sidewalk but I also knew what the bruises looked like.

Pare down. Pare down. Pare down. If you need to buy a suitcase for the trip you may want to try this trick. Lay out all your projected travel accouterment: hairdryer, stockings, makeup, shoes and clothes, travel guides (more about these later) and that all important shower gel you can't live without. Now put the lot into shopping bags, pick up the bags in one hand and try navigating the basement stairs. This is sort of like eating before you go grocery shopping. Common sense takes over. Now go luggage shopping.

You'll need one case to check through to your destination. Don't get a tricky "great idea bag" with little pockets and gadget hidey-holes unless you truly like squirreling away your belongings. I want to unzip and see the whole selection. I want to be able to open, inventory and close with the greatest of ease.

For my carry-on I have a large (22x15") canvas bag. I bought it at a Lands'End outlet store with someone else's monogram on it. I've seen similar bags advertised as boat provision bags, and it works great for lugging groceries into the house. The bag has handles long enough to go over my shoulder but short enough to be carried by the handles without dragging on the ground. In this bag I pack my in-flight goodies: magazines that I haven't had time to read at home, a book, cameras and film, a pair of slippers (fold up ballet type or see the chapter on shoes) and last, but not least, my makeup, comb or brush, toothbrush, toothpaste and medications. If you must, or risk Hell's fire, put in a pair of clean underwear. WARNING! Put the underwear on the bottom of the bag so it doesn't come sailing forth when you grab the camera for a quick shot of the "Welcome to Scotland" sign.

Another little favorite of mine is a ripstop nylon zippered bag that weighs nothing and lies flat on the bottom of my suitcase. If (Ha! I actually said "if") I buy more than I can stuff in my suitcase or mail home, I whip this little bag out and *voila!* I've got another bag for dirty clothes and then the gifts can ride protected in my suitcase. This little bag has traveled with friends to Norway, Russia, Mexico and the East Coast and served admirably, bringing home the spoils of good trips.

LUGGAGE BULLETIN

I am amending this section on luggage with news that I actually made a trip with the next smaller size of "roll around" case and believe you me, that case is now my favorite. No broken shinbones and I directed no rude language toward it. The smaller size also kept me down to a reasonable amount of clothing and -- I still had room for things I never wore.

I'm putting the large case into semi-retirement and perhaps the loaner pool.

Shoes –

Walking and Otherwise

Do not even start packing if you don't have a good pair of "broken-in" walking shoes. Serious walking shoes are a must if you plan on attacking any special interest, including a village ramble. You'll be on your feet more than usual and on uneven ground much of the time. Cobblestones are still much in evidence especially around historic properties. City sidewalks are usually large pavers instead of our familiar poured in place concrete, so you'll meet tippy spots at times and when you start up a worn stone staircase, you'll be grateful for great traction.

A word to the wise, you will always have some sort of walk to your final destination. The car park is usually hidden from the house's view, there is no easy parking along the Royal Mile, and the bus may drop you at the front door but you can bet 50 pence it will be way over there near the cattle barn when it's time to reboard.

There are plenty of attractive walking shoes available now instead of the orthopedic type that gave "walking shoes" a bad name. I still prefer the lace-up variety over the slip-on just because of the stability they give me. They don't have to be expensive. I walked the tread off of a pair of Keds black leather walking shoes and cried when they finally died.

I'd like to suggest not going in those huge, white jogging/athletic/air superstar type shoes. These shoes are worn in Scotland, but usually at the sport that they were invented for – not sightseeing. I always can spot the "American" a mile away because of these boat-sized shoes.

If you are planning to partake in any special interest that requires special shoes, then bring those shoes from home. Hiking and riding boots, tennis and golf shoes, wee dancing slippers or precious little cocktail pumps should be tucked in your suitcase, because some American feet have difficulty in finding a good British or European fit.

If you are lucky enough to find that you do fit the European sized shoes, then this is the time to consider buying flats. They can be dressy, playful, workable, and definitely walkable. Everyone wears flats there.

Summer shoes and sandals should also be walkable and give you support on uneven ground. My sister-in-law found a great pair of good looking sandals by Echo made specifically for walking.

Remember you have places to go and things to see. A turned ankle or blisters can put a mighty big damper on touring.

Wet Feet

Wet feet are a truly ugly thought on vacation when you are away from home and your closet. Think of squishing across the Duchess' pegged oak floorboards after a slog over her lawns to see the Elizabethan kitchen garden. You'll get disdainful looks from the household staff when your shoes ooze and bubble with each step.

In high summer you can tempt fate, but I'd go prepared with the Seattleite's best friend – the "duck shoe" if you are going in any other season. "Duck shoes" are the plastic/rubber molded wonders found in Eddie Bauer and Lands' End type catalogs. You may favor rubber or fabulously expensive, waterproof walking shoes but avoid the malady of wet feet at all costs.

Slippers

I did mention slippers when the carry-on bag was discussed and I promised to mention them again. I love to take my shoes off for the long flight over and back, and stocking feet are at risk from Chicken Kiev droppings in the aisle or even worse in the restroom. I've found a fold-up pair of ballet type slippers are great for that trip to the restroom or pulling your legs up under you while you *try* to sleep.

My friend, Katy, is to be thanked for my felt and cork clogs with a non-slip sole. She raved about hers endlessly and thought the whole office should have a pair. She cut out a newspaper coupon and bought us $6.00 clogs at the local drug store. They are lightweight and comfy. I got on the plane with them packed right on top of my carry-on. Once enroute I slipped off my regular shoes, slipped on my clogs, and gleefully wiggled my toes. An added plus to those clogs - after 8 hours of sitting I didn't have to force my swollen tootsies into too tight shoes. I marched right off the plane in my clogs. These clogs also proved to be great for driving and lounging around.

Packing –

What You Really Need

Don't shop extensively for a new wardrobe. Lay out basics already in your closet. There is nothing worse than finding out those new slacks bind in all the wrong places when you are only a half-hour into the flight.

I like a dark pair of slacks that coordinates with a skirt and jacket, a pair of Levi's or casual slacks and several tops that go with the works. Throw in your dainties and you're done. Yeah right! I know it ain't that simple.

Just make sure that everything goes together. If that fuchsia blouse doesn't go with anything but the Levi's, then you may want to reconsider your options.

Some Tips To Consider

1.   Don't shop extensively before the trip. It's much more fun to shop in Crieff or Inverness.

2.   Coat, Raincoat or Jacket?

You're traveling in which season? You don't want to look like an Eskimo in summer even if you are from Texas and it feels like winter.

I like the zip-out lining raincoat idea for Fall, Winter and Spring. You can be warm or cool with a zip o' the zipper and still look stylish. The raincoat can also serve as a robe if you have to dash down the hall to the bathroom at your B&B.

The height of summer may call for a lightweight jacket that coordinates with your wardrobe.

Why not shop for a cardigan sweater when you arrive in Scotland? Again, buy a color that will be useful on the trip AND when you get home.

3. 	A lightweight, packable dress that goes with the jacket is also a wardrobe stretcher.

4. 	Sleepwear should be warm. I like a flannel-backed, satin gown with a nice pair of bedsocks. Not glamorous, but you'll sleep like a top.

5. 	Cosmetics

Don't take large economy sizes. Experiment with the amount of shampoo you'll use over the time span of your trip. Take only what you need. Repackage into smaller containers and remember most hotels offer the sample sized shampoos in their rooms, but Bed and Breakfasts don't.

6. 	Hair Appliances

Your hairdryer will be useless and fried if you don't have one that offers dual voltage controls. This goes for all North American plug-in appliances. The U.S./Canadian voltage is 110 and the U.K. is 220 and one does not go with the other.

To operate your appliances you will need at least one plug converter. The U.K. and, come to think of it, most of the rest of the world has not caught onto the idea of one standardized plug. Most good travel departments have adapter plugs available. You can go for the Rolls Royce of plug kits that contains a voltage converter along with 3 or 4 plugs (different configurations of prongs or posts) or you can get the triangleish plug with 3 flat prongs that fit in the regular wall outlets for your hairdryer.

A word of warning: I purchased a very expensive voltage converter set and still blew up the converter and my hairdryer. Keep it simple and get a cheap travel, dual voltage hairdryer if you can't survive without one.

Most bathrooms have plugs for "shavers only" so the gentleman of the family can stand upright and shave but you may have to scrunch down in a corner of the room to be near a plug for your hair appliance.

7.   "Casual clothes are de rigueur" says one guide in my collection but just one sentence away the specter of "evening clothes" raises its ugly head. What's going on here? What do you really need to take? Will you actually be having tea with the Duchess of Kent or is it tea in the Duchess of Kent Tearoom?

Be honest with yourself. If you don't have the invitation to the grand, formal ball in your hand don't take the ball gown. If your life at home demands a cocktail dress for dinner at the club with that handsome duffer of yours or if you are planning to attend the Opening Night Gala of the Royal Scottish Ballet, then take one. **One.** Otherwise a nice black skirt or dress that you can dress up or down will be just perfect.

Just remember, you will not be seeing the same people more than a night or two and when you move on that dress you wore in Pitlochry will look new to the crowd in Peebles. If you are on a tour, you'll be in the same boat (or bus) with everyone else and anyway, you won't be worrying about what you're wearing when the pressing issue is deciding between Mixed Grill, Gammon Steak or Courgettes Almondine.

Packing For The Weather

It's time to talk of an indelicate vacation phenomenon - rain. I am a native Seattleite and therefore an authority on the subject. I am not trying to besmirch the sunny brochures put out by the Scottish Tourist Board, but to go unprepared is courting disaster.

Take a small, fold-up umbrella.

Remember in Scotland you are never far from the North Sea or North Atlantic so my best advice is go with the layered look. You can always take a layer or two off when a sudden bright spell overtakes you. In everyday Seattle terms this is the look of comfort; a "look" fashion gurus mistook for a style and named it "grunge." The shirt casually tied around the waist is in reserve for the next micro-climate change. Days can be very warm in mid-summer (August's average temperature is 65 degrees) and all manner of sunburns can be seen on the

Scots, but for a South Carolinian it could mean the start of a nasty cold if chilled on a sweltering 70 degree day.

Take a small, fold-up umbrella.

If you are from the Great Lakes region, you would describe the year round temperature of Scotland as "spring like." Winter's low seldom dips far below freezing and its' highs are in the low forties. Summer's lows are in the forties and the highs are in the sixties and seventies. If the luck of the gods is with you and you do see a truly hot day, you will find the Scots prostrate even to the point of throwing themselves into the frigid sea.

Take a small, fold-up umbrella.

Scottish Tourist Board, please note that I did not mention howling gales, pelting hail, swirling snow or the sudden seaside squall. I have seen them all and thankfully was prepared.

Did I say to pack a small, fold-up umbrella? Think of that umbrella as an insurance policy - if you never have to use it, thank God, but if you need it...

The Purse –

Your Command Center

Before you leave home, let's talk about your purse. I can feel truly superior in this matter because I hate carrying a purse and have never been tempted by giant bags that can haul camping equipment. So here are some tips:

1.   Empty out the bag you are thinking about taking with you. Every item should be removed from every pocket and the crumbs dumped.

2.   Take out of your wallet every single store credit card (Macy's, Nordstrom, Toys R Us), library card, gas card, membership card and store coupons that you cannot use in Scotland.

3.   You won't need your checkbook.

4.   You won't need that huge handful of keys you carry on the miniature jogging shoe keyring. If you must, then extract your house key from the mess and put it in the "to take pile".

5.   Do you really use all that make-up that you carry around and could a smaller hairbrush work for 2 weeks? Could you make do with a lipstick and a comb, putting the rest in your cosmetics bag or in a smaller bag that will fit in your carry-on?

6.   You'll not need your grandson's teething ring, the book of raffle tickets from church, nor the one glove you lost in March.

So how does the "to take pile" look? If you are lucky you have a wallet that is floppy with only your driver's license, credit and debit cards, and maybe a picture of the kids or the dog. You could also have a house key, lipstick, and comb.

Now look at the purse you are planning to take. How much too big is it? Remember you are going to be on your feet and packing that thing for hours at a time. Could you possibly get by with a smaller bag?

I'll now tell you what I carry in my smallish shoulder bag with a strap long enough to wear across my chest. I like this long strapped arrangement because I'm not tempted to set my purse down nor can a light-fingered thief just slip it off my shoulder.

A.   Instead of a floppy wallet, I have found a small ziptop bag, like a small plastic cosmetics bag, serves very well. In that, I carry my credit card, debit card, driver's license, and my British cash. I like this zip top bag because it opens far enough for me to get at the change and the bills without having to extract it from my purse if I don't want to. I have also found that when you are on vacation, coins seem to multiply and never fit into a coin purse.

Once you arrive in Scotland, your American cash can reside in the zipper pocket of your suitcase until your final morning. By separating it from the British you will save a lot of fumbling around.

B.   I honestly only carry one lipstick and a comb in my purse.

C.   My passport and return ticket are crammed into my purse's inside zipper pocket.

D.   I also have room for my smallish 35mm camera and a roll of film.

There is actually a little bit of room left over but I know I'll have a Cadbury Fruit and Nut bar, brochures, flowers in various degrees of decay and handy wipes fluttering around in there before the vacation is over. So my advice to you is don't leave home without emptying out your purse. Your back will thank you.

Packing Maps and Guides

Use everything at your command to glean information but when you get ready to pack, remember how heavy books are and take a leaf from my friend Ingrid's book... literally.

Ingrid and I went to Hungary together several years ago and we'd both found a guide book which we really liked. But we were going to only a few places covered in each book. Ingrid taught me this trick: Tear out (Yes, Sister Superior, I defaced a book) pertinent pages and take them along. Ingrid returns her pages to her books when she gets home but I inserted mine into my trip scrapbook, which I thought was pretty tricky.

Room Reservations

I only have one tried and true rule about room reservations. Make sure you know where you are going to sleep on your first night. You will be cranky with jet lag, stiff and have swollen feet. You will be excited too, but how long will that last when you find the International Society of Aeronautical Engineers has taken up every room for miles around at your first night's destination. Always have your first night's room booked.

I can't say I've always been very smart about my last night's stay but I think I've finally figured out a really good solution to this problem. When I arrive at my destination airport (usually my departure airport too), I look for adjacent airport hotels and stop there first before hitting the road. I book my room for my last night and then I don't have to worry about returning the car or finding transport from town to the airport. I can have a leisurely morning, depending on flight times, and will be dropped at Departure by the hotel shuttle.

I usually end up spending more for my last night's room just for the convenience of being at the airport, but I've found it much less stressful than last minute hustle and hassle.

Your travel agent can help you with lodging around Scotland but remember, agents earn their living from making reservations and most small hotels, guesthouses and B&Bs don't pay commissions. So why not indulge in some research of your own. Make sure you have a budget in mind and the type of accommodation you really need.

Do you long for endless luxury and spa facilities or would the toilet and shower down the hall be just fine?

Do you need big city amenities for shopping, restaurants, and late night entertainment or would a village with a pub set your heart singing?

Do you want to be right in the center of town or is the country/farm life more to your liking?

Use current guidebooks and the recommendations of friends who have traveled recently. I have been surprised, more than once, to find what once was a reasonable and comfortable guesthouse had been given the full "posh" remodel which also included the price list.

Even though I travel on a fairly strict budget, I always try to sneak a splurge or two onto the agenda so I don't feel deprived. I've stayed in 5-star guesthouses featured in newspapers and country houses touted in coffee table books. I have stayed in one or two affordable castles that I actually found in guidebooks, and I've opted for a glass of wine in elegant lounge bars when I actually couldn't afford a room in the castle.

When you have your heart set on a specific historic accommodation, gourmet restaurant, or activity, it is best to make your reservations early. This is especially true if you are going to Edinburgh in August or September when you will be vying for beds and seats with thousands of Edinburgh Festival-goers.

Within the tour sections of this book I have recommended places that I have stayed or with which I am familiar. Addresses, phone numbers and, if they are available, fax numbers are included for each recommendation.

Shopping –
The Golf Widow's Forte

I will not insult you because if we "golf widows" can do one thing truly well - it's shop. The joy of the hunt, the prowl, the smell of a sale is what we love. We're women and we know shopping.

I will not tell you where to shop like most guidebooks. If I come upon a great little place that is truly worth while, I'll mention it in passing but you won't catch me recommending a place to get handmade lace gloves that you must, must have but will never, never wear in Minneapolis.

Every large town and city boasts at least one chain store. My suggestion is not to waste your time wandering among racks if you aren't really in need of a new pair of black slacks. Go in, have a look when you first encounter a department store and then put that experience behind you. The wee local shops are much more fun and someone will actually have time to be interested in you.

Scottish Woollens

As in all shopping, you get what you pay for. Duh! This is equally true when you are shopping for the world-renowned Scottish woolens. You will encounter chain stores that make you feel you've arrived at the seat of all things glorious in wool. Big sale signs abound to lure you in, but you are going to be gifted with my word of warning and you will not lose your head. The Edinburgh Woollen Mill Shop, Pitlochery Woollen Mill Shop, or the Moffat Weavers are chains and they deal in volume and some great deals. If you are falling for something, look it over well, hold it up and look at the inside. If you are going to buy a suit or a sweater, try it on. Often the low price is arrived at by skimping on style and cut. That blazer may look great on the hanger but it could look very boxy and plain on an actual body.

Woollen mill shops can be a wonderful treasure trove of sweaters for the family. Great teenage boy bulky sweaters, trendy little sets for "miss difficult," and the little kid stuff is really fun - scotty dogs and teddies in tartans, and all are within your budget.

Scottish Tartans

Mine's Armstrong. What's yours? Sounds like a great pick-up line to me.

Unless you have always wanted your family tartan in a kilt skirt, or slacks or even a suit, you may want to reconsider if you don't wear pleated skirts or have a "preppy" type wardrobe. You may want to consider a smaller dose of tartan. There are great scarves sized from pocket to shawl and available in polyester (God Forbid!) to cashmere, so soft, that it will almost melt in the rain.

If Uncle Ed is a golfer, there are great hats and even golf and bar towels in tartan. If your Dad is a

MacDonald through-and-through and he can "hoot man" with the best of them at the annual Burn's Night Supper, then you might consider a sports coat or dress slacks… or maybe not. Ask before you bring something home that may never see the light of day outside the closet.

True tartan is an expensive, labor intensive, woven material. Patterns are registered and controlled down to the last warp and woof.

Tartan will last forever with a little care. I can honestly go to my closet and bring out a well-loved Buchanan kilt skirt that I bought in Edinburgh in 1968. If I'd had a daughter, her daughter would be wearing it now.

Something For Your House

Every house needs a present. My last trip transformed my bathroom. I found wallpaper, fabric, a huge tassel for the shower curtain, and even some large greeting cards (Prince Charles' Scottish watercolors) to be framed. If this sounds like fun, go prepared with a plan because being a quarter of a yard short is a real downer.

Shopping Tips

1.   If you sew, don't waste time searching the books for a pattern. Take a photocopy of the back panel of your American pattern and tuck it in a convenient spot so you can just pull it out and have all your notions and yardages right at hand. Some of the little fabric stores have marvelous yard goods that I've never seen at home.

In fact, I think I may be shopping for upholstery on my next trip.

2.   Factory Stores and Outlets do exist in Scotland and the best way to find them in advance is to get in touch with Gill Cutress & Rolf Stricker for a copy of their book *The Factory Shop Guide - Scotland*. Their phone in London is 181.678.0593 and their Website is www.factoryshopguide.co.uk. These guys have listings from office furniture to shoes, top designer cashmere manufacturers to sheltered workshops for the blind. A real must for the dedicated shopper.

3.   You cannot go wrong with the gift of food. There is no size or color choice to be made and no agonizing over modern or traditional china. Look for unusual things like heather honey or whiskey flavored mustard. The worst that will happen is the tin of haggis will end up in your local food bank collection bin.

4.   One thing to remember about those tartan tins of shortbread and jars of gooseberry sauce is that they are heavy to tote around with you. Consider your mode of transport before you go mad at the checkstand. If you have a car, you can fling the stuff in the trunk and never have to touch it again until that final packing job, but if you are on a bus tour, the overhead may not be the place for four pounds of tinned figgy puddin'.

A suggestion: If you are schlepping around the country on the train, bus, bike, or on foot, you may want to leave that final food shopping for your last day. If need be, you can get a taxi to take you to the nearest shop that has what you require and then deliver you right back to the front door of your hotel.

5.   The duty free shop is a terrific place to buy your single malt scotch or for the "old duffer", his favorite bourbon. I would not suggest duty free for your souvenir shopping. The choices are somewhat limited and usually the best-of-the-best brands sporting prices that can make your head spin. I don't understand Rolex on a good day so why would I consider one on my last day in Scotland?

        Every once in awhile on the way to the checkout stand with my bottle of MacAllan 12 year old single malt, I'll spot a commemorative "special purchase" or an extra value item that is just that – a value. Then I may succumb, but I find duty free shops to be pretty depressing when it comes to median priced/good quality gifts.

Getting It Home

So you've splurged and bought everything that wasn't nailed down or found the matching dessert set to Great Aunt Louise's dinnerware. Now how do you get it home? Well over the years I've brought home everything from copper cookware to an antique pub mirror and I have a few tips about the packing or shipping of those "must have" items.

I truly don't know how I collect so much crap when I travel. When I leave home, my little rip stop nylon bag is tucked away for my overflow buying tendencies and I always feel that this will keep me well covered for the return trip but more often than not, I have twice as much stuff as that little bag will hold.

I know I didn't pick up all those flyers and brochures and magazines that weigh a ton. Well, I didn't pick them up all at once. They just got stuffed into a pocket, tucked into my purse, or at the worst, thrown into the back seat of the car. This is truly one of the major drawbacks of a car. You can cart around boxes and shopping bags, leftover lunches and "car food", and those all-important shells you've picked up on the beach in St. Andrews or a rock from the path at Holyrood Palace. It all mounts up. How do your get it home and do you really want it all?

What do you do when you walk down the High Street in Melrose and the winter coat of your dreams just screams out your name? It is on sale, as well as the slacks and jacket that match your entire collection of blouses back home. Add those three items to the chunky sweater for your sister Katy, the antique clock that is perfect for the hall table, and let's not mention the teddy bear wearing a kilt for little Ian. Ack! You're out of control. Who cares?

Not me, in fact, I've been in worse shape than what I've just accused you of being. Here's what you can do to gain some control back.

1.   Sort your brochures, read them, and then discard the ones you don't want and can't imagine why you picked them up in the first place. Rip out the recipes you've found in the newspaper and heave the remainder. Peruse the magazine one more time and leave it for the landlady or rip out the article you can't leave behind. Be ruthless because paper is heavy. You won't believe the amount of paper you can discard when you realize you have to pack it home.

2.   When you've been on a buying splurge at one store, you can have them ship your items home. This can be an expensive option but one you may want to consider if you've got your heart set on a china tea set or delicate crystal flutes. The store will have the proper shipping materials for fragile items and you can make sure they are properly insured for their journey.

3.   **The Trial Pack:** Two days before you are to depart, lay out your treasures and make an honest assessment of the situation. Try a trial pack of your bags. If this leads you to the conclusion that you've had a fabulous time, judging by the stuff you've collected which won't fit into the suitcases or carry-on then you must get ruthless.

Can some of that loot travel without its space gobbling packaging? If the crystal bottle stopper came in a box twice it's size and you can wrap it in your new tartan scarf, then ditch the box. The clear plastic sleeve around the stuffed animal may look protective, but you can fluff Harris Bear's fur with the steam iron when you get home and save a few centimeters of space now.

Pack again. Does it all fit?

Remember to get the cosmetics travel kit from the bathroom and stick that in too. I once had the unhappy experience of having to make space for that at the very last minute. Does it all fit? If not...

4.   **The Box:** Why did God create cardboard boxes? So you can get your treasures home. Any ninny knows that!

As you consider the sad prospect of having to go home, make a trip to the grocery/liquor store or the bar in your hotel and beg a box. Make sure the box is sturdy or get two that can be slipped one inside another. Scavenge some newspapers in the resident's lounge, buy some packing tape and a marking pen at the stationer and you are set to go.

Your aim here is to end up with two pieces of luggage to be checked in at the airport – your suitcase and THE BOX.

Now do a test pack of the suitcase and the box and your carry-on. If it all fits, you are "The Champ" but if it doesn't… well then you've got a problem. Oops, sorry, I've got to run.

How cruel is that?

Okay so let's solve the problem.

Some of the next suggestions may seem really dumb but when it comes to finding space nothing is to be overlooked.

5.   Are all shoes stuffed? Remember, there is room in the stiff toes that can hold socks and other crushables or those cheap little keyrings you bought for the neighbor kids.

6.   Your carry-on bag is a trove of room now that your mail and magazines have been read and discarded, and you don't need that clean set of underwear. When it comes to the carry-on my motto is:

 "It Only Hurts For A Little While"

Your carry-on may just be the best place for that bulky, bronze, sheepdog figurine. I know it is heavy but remember my motto:

 "It Only Hurts For A Little While"

7.   I have actually left old shoes behind and tossed out old underwear that should have been thrown out two years ago.

8.   Take the exposed rolls of film out of their little black canisters and heave the canisters. Take the unexposed film out of their boxes and just pack the canisters. You'd be surprised where these little cylinders can fit.

9.   Consider your traveling costume. Even if it is August, you may want to wear your new bulky hand-knit Aran sweater or the spectacular calf length winter coat you found in Drumnadrochit. Remember the motto and realize that you can strip down once you are on the plane. The welcoming committee will carry your overflow when you get to your destination.

10.   If all else fails there is always the post office just down the street. Remember, weight and waiting really count when posting internationally. You can spend a king's ransom to have your purchases within the week via airmail, but if you are willing to wait 5 to 6 weeks for your treasures, winter coat or dirty laundry then go the slow sea route.

11.   If you have collected rare back issues of *Gardener's Weekly*, art books, or leather bound volumes of Sir Walter Scott's work, ask about the "book rate". You may ship books, and only books, to get this rate.

12.   On your last morning look at your toiletries. If you've traveled with small sized items you have used up

a goodly amount of product. Can you leave the shampoo bottle behind? Can you leave behind the little hotel-sized items you've picked up at several of your stops?

So now we are getting serious.

13.	My next suggestion has to do with the duty free booze you bought on the way to Scotland. I've always bought a bottle of something to carry with me. It is fun to share a drink with a new friend in the Resident's Lounge as you sit in front of a coal fire, or treat your landlords to a drink when they ask you to join them for a rainy evening's TV viewing. I've also enjoyed making myself an evening drink to be enjoyed with a sunset on the sea wall across the street from my bed and breakfast. And for strictly medicinal purposes, a liberal dose of Scotch can knock you right out when you are so tired you think you can't sleep. BUT… What do you do with that 1/3 full bottle? Well you could get blasted on your final night, or invite your fellow travelers for a little 'cheese and drinks do' in the resident's lounge or you can also graciously leave the bottle for your landlady's enjoyment.

You can purchase a new bottle at Duty Free on the way out of the country.

I know this is going to be thought of as sacrilegious by "The Golfer" but… If you are traveling with a golfer, then those beloved clubs are probably snugged up in a pretty snazzy piece of luggage. All those little zipper pockets and the void around the clubs – Bin Laden and his men could hide in there, so why shouldn't you use this space? Now don't put anything around them that would scratch those titanium shafts because you have plans for a trip to Ireland and "The Golfer" must be kept happy.

14. Once you've got your box packed to the gills, give it a good shake to see if anything is rattling around and in need of a wad of newspaper to secure it. Then use the packing tape to securely close the box and protect any weak spots. Remember this box is going to be handled by goons and machinery, so make it secure.

Do not use twine, string, or cord to close or make handles on the box.

Upon arrival at the airport, scout out a luggage cart or trolly immediately and load all of your belongings on it. You will look like a refugee, so there is no use acting chic and world savvy until you've checked your bags with your airline.

Since the events of September 11, 2001 baggage restrictions are ever changing so check with your travel agent or airline for their up to the minute rules on luggage.

Scots Fare – The fanfare please!

TAA DAA Ta DAAAA!!!

The food in Scotland is better than ever! I must admit the past 10 years have seen a remarkable change in the quality of Scottish cuisine. In fact, "cuisine" was not a word you would have heard in Scotland except when a vacation to France was being discussed.

Around every corner you can find yummy cheap eats and expensive, gourmet meals, where once you could only find the soggy chip, mushy pea and sauced mystery meat at every price point. Fresh vegetables and aged meats are no longer oddities, and arteries can be heard healthily pumping for their lack of fried food.

Breakfast still leans heavily on the hearty traditional English Breakfast, or just "full breakfast" in many places. This usually involves juice or tinned fruit, corn flakes or numerous other dry cereals, eggs, sausage, bacon, broiled tomato and toast with real butter and marmalade. Depending on the landlord's flair in the kitchen, you may find muesli, hot porridge, kippers, blood pudding, haggis or an omelet on the menu. No matter what is offered, you will not go away hungry.

I usually go heavy on the juice and fruit and order my eggs scrambled with grilled tomato and a slice of bacon. I try to stay away from the toast but it is the best way to get the butter into my mouth, so I usually have at least a slice from the toast rack. Once I overdose on butter, I ask that the toast not be brought to the table.

Lunch can be a great sit down affair in one of Edinburgh's fine old department stores, or as simple as a hunk of cheese and crackers from the specialty cheese shop. I like to find "salad sandwiches" that are served in many bakeries along with homemade soups. The famous

"Pub Lunch" is filling and a fabulous value but may leave you wanting a snooze too early in the day.

Dinner is an adventure, whether you find the bistro tucked down an alley that serves exquisite crepes or the chain of decent Italian restaurants that has sprung up around the country. Indian, Chinese, Greek, American burger joints, Irish, and the well-loved neighborhood fish and chip shop will tempt you to try their wares. The choices of restaurants are now as varied as the dishes they serve and that makes the nightly choice difficult.

Prices can be rather high in the nicer restaurants and hotels, so ask to see the menu before you are seated, just in case bread and water are not on your hit parade for the next three nights.

If you can squeeze your budget tightly enough, try eating at a restaurant that belongs to the "Taste Of Scotland" scheme. These establishments meet stringent guidelines and use only the freshest produce, seafood, meat and dairy products that Scotland produces and the price reflects this quality. The dishes are usually unique, beautifully presented and served in elegant or charming surroundings. This would be well worth a Mars candy bar lunch the next day.

Don't confuse a "Taste of Scotland" meal with a Scottish Night Out meal. The latter's food is usually cranked out in mass for a crowd of tourists who are there to sing *"Scotland the Brave"*, hear a pipe skirl and see a kilt twirl. These are fun evenings but not usually your gastronomic adventure.

Television cooking shows are extremely popular in Scotland and there are even several game shows based on innovative cooking. I'm sure we will be seeing them on this side of the pond after the success of *The Weakest Link* and *Survivor*.

All in all you won't be disappointed with Scot's fare and you may even go home with something new to try on the other golfers and their widows.

Car Rental Tips and Driving On The Wrong Side

Arrange for your car before you leave home and preferably on the day you get your airline reservations. Depending on the season, style availability can be limited. I was once upgraded into a lovely estate car (station wagon) without extra charge because they were out of the type of car I had reserved. I wouldn't mind driving a Jaguar on a free upgrade but somehow I don't think that would happen. If I had to pay for a Jag, my budget would be shot and sleeping in a Jag is just not cool.

Discuss your car needs with yourself, or if you are traveling with "the golfer" or a girlfriend, involve them in the decision, whether they will be driving or not.

What size of car will you need? I find a subcompact works just fine for one and may work for two if you are close friends and not exceedingly tall or wide.

Will you feel comfortable with a standard transmission or is an automatic a must? The standard transmission will be operated with your left hand so that may be something to consider. It isn't difficult but can be fairly embarrassing the first day or two, especially if the rental guy is standing right there and you can't find first gear.

Your travel agent can help you with reservations or you can shop around. The major worldwide rental agencies are widely represented but there are British and small local agencies as well. Shop the rates of all of them – you may be pleasantly surprised with the differences.

If you are planning on spending your first few days in Glasgow or Edinburgh remember, parking is absolutely the pits. Consider not picking up your car until you are ready to leave for the countryside. Public transport in and around cities is marvelous and even a brisk walk can bring you to unexpected delights that would be totally missed while driving.

Another advantage of not having a car the first few days is that by the time you are ready to pick up your car, you'll have almost been run over three or four times because you looked the wrong way at a cross walk. With this fear of imminent death, you will look both ways (just like your mom always told you) before pulling out into traffic at the rental agency's parking lot.

Driving on the "Wrong Side" can be a daunting thought to the first timer but it really isn't that difficult. I have driven American, left hand drive cars in Britain and that is difficult and extremely dangerous.

Remember <u>everything</u> is backwards. Not only are you driving on the wrong side of the road but you are sitting on the wrong or, should I say, the right side of the car to drive. Just like home, when you are in the driver's seat you'll be next to the centerline of the road. See - just backwards.

So here are some exercises to try at home. Pull two chairs up to the kitchen table (side-by-side), pretend this is the front seat of your car and the edge of the table is the dashboard. Use a dinner plate for the steering wheel. Now, find a ribbon or cut paper strips to replicate a centerline. Place the centerline on the table to the right and parallel to what would be the driver's door. You now have your car and your lane stretching out in front of you. It is time to engage your imagination.

Using the driver's side door, get into the driver's seat. Look at the centerline just to the right of the driver's side door and prepare to move into traffic. Use your blinker and look behind you for traffic. Did you look over your right shoulder at the oncoming traffic or over your left into the back seat? See, it's just backwards. As long as you are conscious of where that centerline is, you've nearly got "wrong side" driving licked.

You can create all sorts of scenarios with more ribbon or paper strips.

Make an intersection and try making right turns and then left turns. Think about the centerline and where it should be when you've completed the turn and in which direction traffic is flowing. Once you've mastered the intersection you are ready to move on to The Roundabout.

In all but the newest motorways, which now have overpasses or cloverleaf interchanges, the British highway system relies on the roundabout to direct and distribute traffic. The roundabout is like a bicycle wheel's hub and the converging roads are like spokes on the wheel. You will get early warnings when you are approaching a roundabout and accompanying signage will show you which road to take out of the roundabout. Many also have speed warnings and some will have speed bumps because you may have to come to a complete halt before entering the roundabout.

Now how do you enter the roundabout? Slow down and look to your right for oncoming traffic. All traffic will be going in the same direction in the roundabout.

Enter the traffic flow using the outside lane of the roundabout. Faster vehicles and those going farthest around the roundabout move toward the center. There is a lot of lane switching and what seems like terrible chaos.

When I first start driving, I usually stay in the outside lane so I can drive a little slower and read the exit signs as they whiz by. Don't feel like a loony if you have to drive around twice before you find your exit. Just think of the extra trip around as insurance in choosing the right route.

When leaving the roundabout, I've found it wisest to aim for the left hand lane of your exit because the road you are entering may be a two way street and you don't want to meet someone coming head on.

Politeness is a key, eye contact helps, and use your turn signals. It can feel like you are entering a whirlwind depending on the traffic so keep your wits about you and after a few experiences you'll be an old hand.

I know this feels like you are 15 again and getting your learner's permit but remember that a little bit of time spent on these pretend exercises will get you down some really amazing roads.

If you are still unsure about driving, I have included a chapter, 10 Days Without A Car, later on in the book. It will take you from Historic Edinburgh to Cosmopolitan Glasgow, and as far north as Inverness and even stopping in St. Andrews for a look at the hallowed ground of golf.

Returning The Rental Car

Like I've said before, I like to spend my last night at an airport hotel so I'm not surprised by unexpected traffic or road construction on departure day. I drive right up to the hotel and transfer my luggage to my room. Then I move the car to the carpark for that last search for belongings that may have shifted under the seat or been forgotten in the glove box. Don't forget to check the CD player.

If I have any last minute touring or a dinner down the road, then I can do that before turning in my car at my leisure. Depending where the rental return facility is, I can walk, or take the rental car shuttle over to the departure terminal where I check with my airline to see if they are anticipating any delays and to get their recommended check-in time.

Now that you are car free, just find your hotel's shuttle and hit the bar.

My Daily Schedule

I throw out my regular at-home schedule starting the first morning of my trip. I feel obligated to get the most out of my day without exhausting myself because my vacations are just too short to lollygag around.

Start the day with a good breakfast, which is usually included in the price of your lodging. Don't say,

"I'll just have toast and coffee." Besides the fact the coffee is usually dismal, you'll need fuel to get you tromping over hill and dale not to mention the Duke's parquet floor.

You'll see "morning coffees" advertised in cafés and many bakeries, and now Starbucks is popping up on larger city street corners. Take advantage of these and of the village shop for a bottle of juice or water so you don't get dehydrated. That cup of tea, juice, soda or beer is very important to your well being. This may sound elemental but you'll be very surprised how thirsty you can get when the faucet isn't right there.

Hold off having lunch until 1:30ish or so, and then have a late afternoon/early evening snack before partaking in my most unusual trip activity - Nap Time. After I've worn my feet to nubs from tromping over paving stones and cobbles, up spiral stairs, across marble floors, down into musty crypts and skipping (or is that tripping?) over rubble walls, I get settled into my room. I take my shoes off and put my feet up, have a cuppa, turn on the telly or pick up a book or magazine and relax. I don't nap well but I find just putting my feet up is the next best thing. You can also use this "nap time" for tomorrow's planning session and washing out a few things. Don't feel guilty about being in your room and not being "out there." Rest up, wash off the day's grime, and put on a new face. You have time before dinner because if you go to dinner at 5 or 6pm, you'll often be the only one in the dining room or restaurant. Go later and you'll have plenty of company in the room and you can engage in some great people watching. 7:30 to 8:30pm is my target dinnertime.

Now you know the reason for the late afternoon snack.

If you've ferreted out a "ceilidh" or Scottish Night Out at the nearby social hall or a lecture sponsored by the Women's Institute, the starting time will be later than earlier and most events will have refreshments available. Some of my favorite evenings have been standing around the tea table tasting the homemade goodies and exchanging recipes.

When I get back to my B&B or hotel, I always stick my head into the Resident's Lounge and see who's there. You may bat zero and find everyone is tucked up tight for the night or you may share experiences late into the night with a fellow traveler. If you've seen something unusual or fun during your day, don't hesitate to mention it because they may have seen something you would have never found. You might also find someone who is dying to see the Kelvingrove Art Museum and Park as much as you are.

The best schedule is one that can be massaged to take advantage of what may present itself. Would you really kick yourself around the block if you didn't see the "Glasgow Boys" exhibit? Then see it. BUT if a day at the horse races jumps up and presents itself to you on a glorious sunny day, then that just might be the ticket to some novel fun you couldn't get back home. Go with the flow and be flexible.

A Safe Evening Out

Looking for a safe place for an evening out? Ask your landlady or lord, the bank teller, or the book shop owner. Again use your intuition.

I wouldn't ask the kid with the tattoos but I know some of you would. He may know some great places; but would his scene's music drive me mad within minutes? Or worse yet why would a "Golf Widow" want to frequent a pub where all eyes are focused on the Match of the Day? Been there! Done that! Slap one of the glazed-over patrons out of his football reverie and find out where the wives are. You'll usually find they are not far away and I bet there will be no "telly" with football and the room will be lively.

If you feel uneasy about walking and the evening's entertainment isn't just around the corner, then call a taxi. The hotel or your landlady would be only too happy to help you make the call.

If you really want some fun look for the pubs with "Quiz" notices on their sidewalk sandwich boards or in the window. This is serious fun. It's like a game show where patrons go up against one another, individually or on teams. The competition eventually goes pub against pub and town against town. It's cutthroat and witty with the audience having as much fun as the participants. If you want to take part, then read the local newspaper, watch the television news, and listen to the radio because current events are major components of each quiz.

Not into the pub scene every night? Then here are some more ideas:

1.   Scottish Nights are usually held in hotels or restaurants and are often out-of-date tourist attractions that feature schmaltzy music from grandma's era, dance and often a sing-a-long just for good measure. The show is usually put on by a professional group of entertainers and there may be dinner involving haggis in some form. Fun for a one-of sort of thing but I much prefer ...

2.   Ceilidhs (Kaylees) are traditional gatherings and now come in many different forms. Here in Seattle, a Ceilidh is held after the closing ceremonies of our Pacific Northwest Highland Games and it comes very close to the small town ceilidhs I've attended in Scotland. Young and old participate, on equal footing, in the evening's entertainment and there is often a competition for best talent. You will see and hear just about anything. I've seen a 5 year-old violinist knock the socks off the cocky, middle-aged crooner, and a belly dancer get a standing ovation over the highland dancer's polite applause. Many small local ceilidhs go hand-in-hand with a dance, a late supper (sandwiches and desserts), and the ever present

bar for false courage if you want to get up and strut your stuff.

3.   Larger towns usually have cinemas so you can catch up on your movies.

4.   Check out shop windows for local events that may be going on at the church hall or the seaman's lodge. You'll be surprised at the scope of the offerings. Everything from academic lectures, local theatre companies, or a traveling, world-class string quarter may be in the close vicinity.

5.   Television offers up entertainment too and you can soak your swollen feet at the same time. *Antiques Roadshow* had its beginnings in Britain and had been on the telly for years before the New World discovered it. The "stuff" is just different. The old Civil War sword isn't from the 1860s but from the 1640s. People everywhere react the same way when they learn that the old table from the front hall is worth a fortune or that great grannies' diamond necklace is a fake.

Game shows have always been big in Britain and some of you may be surprised to learn that *Who Wants to be a Millionaire* and *The Weakest Link* came to us after seasons of successes in Britain.

One of my favorite game shows is the one where neighbors or best friends redo rooms in each other's homes. The rules, timelines, and budgets are strict, designers and carpenters help the contestants so the results are professional, and the reactions are hilarious.

I've seen tears of joy or the absolute end of friendships when the contestants are ushered into their new rooms. There is now a facimile of this show on one of our cable stations but it is mild by comparison.

6.   If you are in a town with a college or university stop by the front office and find out what is on the schedule. This stop could lead to some very interesting networking if you find something being offered in your realm of expertise.

7.   Bowling. Hey, quit laughing. Bowling is back and you can find bowling alleys in larger cities.

8.   Bingo. Hey, quit laughing at that idea. Bingo has never been out of fashion in Britain and the bingo halls are packed.

9.   Leisure Centres. These centers are among the newest buildings in town and cover a full range of exercise and sport facilities. Depending on the center, you could find swimming pools, hot tubs, massage facilities, gyms, tennis courts, banks of exercise machines, and even beauty salons. So you could treat your evening like a spa vacation and go home looking like a million bucks. Drop in early in the day for a schedule, visitor information, and a list of services available. If you need to make appointments it may be best to do it as soon as possible in the day, as these centers are extremely popular. Many leisure centres have facilities for light meals and even bars to help replace those calories you have just worked off.

10.   Each and every town and village will have their own special evening entertainment and folks from miles around will come to enjoy them. Here are a few: miniature golf, dry slope skiing, free dance lessons in pubs (from Scottish Country to American Cowboy Line to the Brazilian samba), indoor, artificial rock climbing cliffs, archery and snooker.

The local Tourist Office, your landlord, and the local paper will all have some information for evening entertainments.

Admission Fees

It is difficult to give firm prices on admission fees, excursions and events, so I've decided to give you some price range guides instead.

If an attraction has an admission fee, that fee's price range will be noted by dollar signs after the word "Fee".

$ =   Less than $5.00 US
$$ = $5.00 to $8.00 US
$$$ = $8.00 US and above

Substantial savings can be made by purchasing memberships in organizations or combined admission tickets to an organization's properties. Memberships offer free admission to members and a combined ticket allows you to make one purchase for several properties. Either way, you'll save money and avoid waiting in lines to purchase tickets.

These admission packages are wonderful for the first-time visitor or for the traveler seeking an in-depth look at Scotland's best properties. The following Organizations offer memberships and combined tickets:

Historic Scotland, Longmore House, Salisbury Place, Edinburgh EH9 1SH, Ph 131.668.8830 or www.historic-scotland.gov.uk.

 The National Trust for Scotland, 5 Charlotte Square, Edinburgh, EH2 4DU, Ph. 131.226.5922.

The Great Houses of Scotland, Blair Castle, Pitlochry, PH18 5TL, 179.648.1207.

You can make an advance purchase before leaving home, or purchase your membership or combined ticket at the first visit to an attraction that is a member of the scheme. All of the schemes have nice brochures and they can be requested from the Tourist Board.

So let's get going. Time is a wasting and we have some traveling to do.

~3~

The Quiet Southwest Galloway and Dumfries

The Birthplace of Many a Golf Widow

The Golf Courses:

Powfoot and Portpatrick (Dunskey)

Long, long ago and far away, before titanium shafts and "Big Bertha", fairies, witches, golden swans, and beautiful ladies inhabited the shires of Galloway and Dumfries. All was peaceful and a world unto its own, where even wee hobbits would have been comfortable, until one day the evil Southern Kingdom passed a law which lead to the creation of hundreds of new golf widows.

Gretna Green – Where Golf Widows may first have been created.

In 1753, England passed a law requiring marriage age without parental consent to be raised to 21 and the rush was on to the town of Gretna Green just across the border in Scotland. In Scotland, young lovers, very young lovers, could still marry at 16 with no license or minister required – just someone to receive their public plight of troth before the parents, who were usually in hot pursuit, arrived to stop the marriage. The legal age in Scotland is still 16 but licenses and a minister are now required by law.

Gretna Green's <u>Old Blacksmith's Shop</u> became the most popular wedding spot because the main road from England ran right past the front door and the smithy was always in.

Beautiful ladies in long flowing gowns can still be seen in this "romantic heart of Scotland". As they are happily stepping up to the anvil altar, unaware that the groom has way too many golf courses on his mind.

Behind the Blacksmith Shop is a lovely, recently added sculpture garden (perfect for those wedding snapshots) with a sheltering surround of tasteful shops, two restaurants and, I swear, the cleanest and largest ladies room I've ever seen. I'm tempted to take photos and send them to the major sporting and cultural venues here in my hometown where I've spent plenty of time waiting in the ladies room line.

Joke weddings are performed for tour groups, but highly planned affairs are now the norm and Gretna Green offers all the services needed for that special wedding day. Weddings Without Worries will do the planning; William Woodhouse, Photographer, will record the day, the Anvil Bar provides reception space, and bridal suites are available "upon request" at Lover's Leap Lodges. The florist shop, just off the sculpture garden, offers posies, but elaborate bouquets need 24 hour advanced notice. What could be easier than this one stop shopping? For my money the Gretna Hall Hotel (Gretna, DG16 5DY, Ph. 146.133.8257) looks like a place that would make all the arrangements for you. Gretna Hall, built in 1710 has its original "smithy" in the back garden so no tour groups will be tromping through those "special day" photos.

And what could be nicer for those bridal couples than a honeymoon on the golf course? If you play golf that would be terrific but if you don't then being the caddy in your wedding trousseau is probably not what you had in mind for that romantic honeymoon.

So here we are again at the reason for this book. Leave that golfer behind, get out there and make some fun for yourself. He'll be okay and once on the course swappin' tales, he won't even see you clickin' your heels.

Galloway and Dumfries

Not many tourists find this part of Scotland. This is not Edinburgh, nor The Highlands, and not even The Islands. There are few tartan/souvenir shops and tour buses don't clog the byways. Towns are small and surrounded by beautiful pastureland with some of Britain's finest dairy herds grazing contentedly. Besides these bucolic vistas, there are many unusual things to see and do here but a car is a must. Train service is spotty and bus service offers a lazy schedule usually aimed at local day shoppers.

But first, a WARNING!

This quiet corner of Scotland is intersected by the A75 highway from Gretna Green to Stranarer on the Irish Sea. Since the advent of the European Union this road has become one of the most dangerous in Britain. Huge, speeding trucks, carrying the commerce of the E.U., barrel down this road trying to make the ferry in Stranarer or the early markets in London. Keep your head about you, skip the beer at lunch and you should be fine.

Powfoot

One of my "first nights" in Scotland was spent in Powfoot, a village not bigger than a blink of the eye. Powfoot's major claim to fame was winning Britain's Small Village Award for it's tidy appearance and meticulously tended yards which attest to the semi-tropical climate of this part of Scotland. There is a small golf course here which isn't famous, nor is it particularly challenging, but it is quiet, rising and falling on very green, bumpy hills along the Firth of Solway. The adjoining hotel, The <u>Powfoot Golf Hotel</u> (Powfoot, Dumfriesshire DG12 5PN, Ph.146.170.0254 00254, Fax 146.170.0288) boasts turf fires tended by a friendly, young staff, a lounge bar that puts out a great meal, and best of all, a great big bath tub – extra long and plenty of hot water. This place is a fine spot to spend a first night or a quiet layover to regroup. Take a long beach walk before breakfast and then away you go, onto another adventure.

Caelaverock

Caelaverock <u>National Nature Reserve</u> didn't sound like my cup of tea but I'd been told it was a "grand" place to stop. Indeed it was.

In the parking lot, I booted up next to a man unpacking an exceedingly large camera and tripod. We chatted and he invited me to join him on the trail to the blind where he was to be looking for some elusive and rarely seen bird.

The first stop, after entering what appeared to be a farmyard, was a flimsy looking wooden building that protected a series of ponds from the parking lot and the farmyard. Once inside, two levels of windows opened onto the ponds and it was a true "Kodak moment". A naturalist was on duty to take the tickets and talk about the current residents of the wildlife reserve. He pointed out curved-beaked curlews, teal, red-eyed oystercatchers and hundreds of whooper swans resting here before flying on to a Norwegian summer.

My photographer friend didn't even take the lens cap off so I expected he was after something ever more wonderful. Down the trail we went, out onto what I'd call a delta. Blinds were carved out for observation and I was able to see tiny roe deer and rabbits galore. The naturalist had been out earlier placing wooden frames around prints in the mud and labeling them. I've never seen a badger but I've seen his print.

At the end of the trail was a wooden fort-like structure that we quietly clambered up and into. Two other photographers were there already. Muffled greetings and wildlife updates were passed and then there was silence. The wait for the grey heron was on. I waited, but then I decided watching the nesting barn owls on closed circuit TV back at the farm house was better than freezing to death. I was right, too. Those little devils are darned cute.

Kirkcudbright (sounds like Kirk-koo-bree)

Kirkcudbright has hosted a lively arts community since the earliest days of the 20th Century. A

Lord Peter Whimsey mystery novel, *Five Red Herrings*, was set here and involved local characters and art world crime in the 1920s. Today the town is alive and well with an arts center, museum, workshops and studios producing and displaying a wide array of fine art and craft.

Tolbooth Arts Centre features a display of local historical and modern arts and crafts. Exhibits change monthly and classes are advertised.

Broughton House was the home of one of the "Glasgow Boys", E.A. Hornel, painter extraordinaire. Today the house is furnished in 17th Century antiques and lavishly hung with Mr. Hornel's 19th and 20th Century paintings. There is, as incongruous as it may seem, a small Japanese garden that was developed after the painter had an extended visit to Japan.

Both of these attractions are located on High Street and direction signs are well placed on the main road. Also on this street I found 3 shops that especially pleased me: Cranberries specialized in arts and crafts, Jo Gallant, Textile Artist and Katherine King, a jewelry maker.

If you want to try your hand at watercolor or oils call Linda Mallet at Kirkcudbright Painting Holiays. She offers up short courses for all levels of expertise in the open air or studio.

Not far from Kirkcudbright is Loch Ken, an inland lake, which hosts the Galloway Sailing Centre. If you've always wanted to learn to sail or windsurf, this is your chance and your bumbles will be done out of sight of friends and neighbors back home. They have a list of courses and a new lodge right at the lake.

Gatehouse of Fleet

So far my travels had kept me off the A75 but to get into Gatehouse, you must cross the highway. Luckily this section of highway has been well planned and is not dangerous.

This once bustling cotton mill town now plays host to year-round visitors who visit the Mill of Fleet to learn how cotton became this pretty little town's livelihood. Cotton and Scotland? Now how does that work?

Gatehouse of Fleet is a wonderful stopping place for a picnic. The town's new car park boasts plenty of space and it adjoins the town's park where picnickers relax, tourists use the new information kiosk and restrooms. A big plus is the adjacent grocery store and a great gift shop/cafeteria. Pick up lunch and head for the park's picnic tables or take your meal to the castle.

Cardoness Castle, just outside of town, is an elegant four story, Scottish tower house built in the 1400s.

The cows at the Cream o'Galloway Dairy aren't the only reason for taking the factory tour. This little factory's motto is "from cow to cone" and they produce high quality ice cream and yoghurt. They have the usual flavors but you may want to try honey oatmeal, whisky, or elderflower. You can picnic on their 80 acres or just belly up to a bowl of heaven.

If I had a special gift to give – wedding, baby, or just because – I'd look up Jean Clements and see her exquisitely creative and playful needlework cushions. They are done with patchwork, silk thread and loving detail. Her "white on white" creations are meltingly beautiful with just a sparkle of pearl and glass beadwork.

Holy Cairns

Venturing back onto the A75, west bound, I passed sign after sign pointing to ruins springing up in fields, but a small sign off to the right pointing to Holy Cairns caught my interest. Sure enough, after a steady climb up a nice road that soon turned into a rutted dirt lane, I found the eerie cairn stones (ancient grave stones) in a fenced pasture. The holy dead rested in a grave with a fabulous view out to the Irish Sea. These stones, standing upright or tilted, are weird and here you are all by yourself with the wind, and the cows, and all this history.

You know what else was weird about this place? Backing out of the car park I caught sight, in my rear view mirror, of a professionally gilded sign announcing "Katherine Ard, Jeweller. As seen in Liberty and

Harrods". The sign pointed up the hill. "Why not?" I said. I had to wait for a tractor to bump its way down before I started up, praying I wouldn't bottom out on one of the large boulders that had been uncovered by winter rains. When I pulled into the farmyard at the top of the hill, a very surprised woman came out of the farmhouse. By the state of the road, I'd guess she didn't get many visitors.

Katherine Ard invited me into her studio, a tiny little greenhouse/shed that was filled with sparkling beads and silver fittings. I bought earrings made with handmade beads from the 1930s, and I remember Katherine's shocked face every time I see those beads swinging from my dear friend Marilyn's ears.

Who would have guessed that just past the dead guys there was a jeweller waiting for a visitor. Now that's why I travel!

NOTE: Katherine has lived all over the world and she was talking about another move so who knows where you'll find her sign.

Wigtown

Back on the A75 again, I chose to make another diversion off into the countryside. After passing through Newton Stewart, which seems to be the hub of industry and commerce for the surrounding villages, I headed south on the A714 out into a land unknown to me. A land where they burned witches and ancient standing stones share land with the Cradle of Christianity.

I pulled into Wigtown, a market town with 2 main streets, North Main and South Main, divided by a small strip of park. Arriving late in the evening I bit the bullet and tried a B&B that didn't look at all appealing from the street. Glaisnock House (20 South Main St., Wigtown DG8 9EH, Ph. 198.840.2249) is run by two semi-retired publicans, Bill and Lydia Cairns. The welcome was hearty and the rooms were well decorated. I really felt bad that I didn't have dinner in the plain little dining room that opened to the street because breakfast there was fabulous. I'm sure what I had assumed to be an overly ambitious dinner menu was marvelous too. Ack well! It was my loss.

Bill served that breakfast up with great good cheer and interesting ideas for the day. He even introduced tables to one another and started us talking. When I discovered I had problems with my computer, Bill sprang into action, found the local computer guru, and I was repaired in no time. Oh yeah, I almost forgot that when I loaded my suitcase into the trunk of my car, Bill spotted my Caelaverock muddied boots and wouldn't hear of me striking out until they were polished. I would stay here again without hesitation for these folks are true hospitality experts.

I did have dinner down the road at the Fordbank Country House Hotel (Bladnoch, Wigtown, Ph: 01988

402346), a large house sitting in its own grounds. he place was empty but I followed the audio from a TV in the basement pub where I found a gang of rabid football fans and the hotel staff. I was settled into the lounge bar upstairs and served a drink when in walked an older couple also wanting a meal. We shared a table and enjoyed each other's company while the meal and the service revolved around the game downstairs. The crowd dispersed and roared out of the car park the moment their team lost and we three diners ended up the evening in quiet comfort with the staff to ourselves.

The Fordbank also seems to be the headquarters for <u>Galloway Country Sports</u> where you can procure fishing permits and tackle.

Witches, and Druids, Saints, and royal pilgrims lived and traveled extensively on this lovely green peninsula. They left behind their unusual legacy for our contemplation.

North Main Street of Wigtown peters out into a narrow lane called Bank Street. Just down a small hill, you will pass the church where the witches or Martyrs of Wigtown are buried. If you keep going to the bottom of the hill and turn into the dirt parking lot, you can walk out a long boardwalk to a simple monument – a stone stake. At one time Wigtown Bay came up to this point and offending "witches" were simply tied to a stake at low tide to stand in terror as the tide came in and drowned them. That's what you got in 1685 for disagreeing with the town fathers and the church.

From Wigtown drive straight down to the end of the peninsula to Whithorn, the seat of the first Christian community in Scotland, thus the name "Cradle of Christianity". You'll be following the route Scottish Kings, assorted royals, and simple pilgrims traveled as a penance to worship in <u>St. Ninian's Cave</u>, a 4th Century cell.

In the town of Whithorn itself, ancient crosses collected in the area have been preserved at the <u>Whithorn Trust Discovery Centre</u>. Near the archaeological dig is an 8th Century settlement and a Viking encampment, both of which show you the wide progression of this area's history.

Your pagan side will feel right at home here as there are standing stones round every bend (it seems like it, anyway). "Wren's Egg" is the only one prominent enough to get named on the map but you'll see little signs all along the way pointing toward ancient sites in farmers' fields.

Just off the A747 in a village called Mochrum, you'll find a Norman castle (11th Century) in fairly good repair. It sits on a motte (mound) to offer a view of the surrounding countryside and approaching enemies.

Back onto the A75 and 3 miles east of Stranraer, the Kennedy family didn't keep an eye open and in 1716 their castle burned. Today <u>Castle Kennedy</u> is the site of a luscious garden. Situated between two lakes, the garden sports the well placed ruin and a "new" house (Lochinch Castle). A most spectacular avenue of rhododendrons and azaleas steals the show in May.

Stranraer

Located on the sheltered Loch Ryan, Stranraer is home port for the ferries to Northern Ireland. This is not a picture postcard place but because of the ferry traffic, it is a great place to find a room. I've stayed here and taken the early ferry to Larne. Back then, our landlady didn't get up to see us off but there were steaming carafes of coffee and tea and rolls waiting in the dining room.

Stranraer, 2 1/2 hours from Glasgow by train, is located on the rugged Rhinns of Galloway Peninsula that stretches out into the Irish Sea. The Rhinns, mountainous hills, snake down the peninsula and offer precipitous cliff views and tiny sandy beaches. The area enjoys some of the most moderate weather in all of Britain because of the Gulf Stream. This may explain the proliferation of gardens that are open to the public.

Ardwell House Gardens surround a lovely country house (not open to the public) which presents an idyllic backdrop for the plantings. Rhodies, azaleas, bulbs and border plants are the focus here. A garden shop offers plants for sale and in season you can "u-pick" strawberries. Find a bottle of wine and a tub of sour cream and you're all set for a blazing sunset over the Irish Sea.

Logan Botanical Gardens, a specialist garden for the Royal Botanical Garden in Edinburgh, capitalizes on the mild climate with semi-tropical plants, tree ferns and cabbage palms. If you are visiting in the colder months this is a strange place indeed. You'll feel like you are visiting paradise in your parka.

Drive down to the very end of the road on the Rhinns of Galloway Peninsula (south of Stranraer) and you'll reach the bleak and windswept Mull of Galloway with spectacular views ranging from Belfast, Northern Ireland to Hartlepool, England. The cliffs here support thousands of nesting seabirds.

The Southern Upland Way, Scotland's longest footpath, starts at Portpatrick, a small resort village to the south west of Stranraer. If you chose to stroll this path to its very end, you'd walk the entire Border Region of Scotland and end up 212 miles away in Cockburnspath on the North Sea. The whole walk takes between 10 and 20 days to traverse but the Way is accessible along its route, so even an afternoon's walk could be planned. Be prepared with good hiking shoes and a daypack because this is Scotland and the weather can change on a dime (or should I say a 10p?).

Little Portpatrick also has an unusual golf course. Portpatrick (Dunskey) is a links-type course that perches on the cliffs above the sea instead of on the beach. This is a great place to park a golfer while you visit the gardens and ancient sites on the Rhinns of Galloway Peninsula.

Lodging – Stranraer & Vicinity

Balyett Farmhouse B & B (Cairnryan Road, Stranraer DG9 8QL, Ph. 177.670.3395) is a working farm. You've been driving past some of the finest dairy farms in Britain so you might as well see how these farms work. Farming also means early-to-work so that means the cook will be up and a hot breakfast will be ready before the ferry. Am I shallow or what?

The Lighthouse Hotel (Kirkcolm, Stranraer DG9 0QG, Ph. & Fax 177.685.4231), once a lighthouse keeper's house and barns, is now a posh little inn sitting right next to the still working lighthouse. The 20 acre property is stunning and you are welcome to wander.

For the more budget minded try Aislie View Guest House (8 Agnew Crescent, Stranraer, Ph. 177.670.5792) which is right downtown and faces Loch Ryan but is just far enough away from the traffic and trains to be quiet.

Carlton Guest House (South Crescent, Portpatrick DG9 8JR, Ph. 177.681.0253) is right on the seafront.

Southwest Diversions –

Hours & Directions

Old Blacksmith's Shop Centre, Gretna Green DG16 5EA, Ph. 146.133.8441 is ten miles north of Carlisle or 15 miles south of Locherbie. Watch for the brown tourist attraction signs. Open daily, 9am-5pm in the winter and longer hours in spring, summer and fall. There is a fee ($) to enter the Blacksmith's Shop but the other facilities are free.

Caelaverock National Nature Reserve, Wildfowl & Wetlands Trust, Eastpark Farm, Caerlaverock DG1 4RS. Follow the "Solway Coast Heritage Trail" signs on the A75 if you are traveling west from Annan or the "Wildfowl Trust" signs from the eastbound A75 in Dumfries. Open daily 10:00am-5:00pm except Christmas. Fee $$.

Caelaverock Castle and the offices of Scottish Natural Heritage are very near the Nature Reserve and well worth visiting.

Tolbooth Arts Centre, High Street, Kirkcudbright. Open year round Mon-Sat, times vary but usually 11:00am to 5:00pm. Longer hours in summer and some Sundays. Fee $.

Broughton House, 12 High Street, Kirkcudbright. Open April-Oct, daily 1:00pm-5:30pm. Fee $$.

Kirkcudbright Painting Holiays, 49 Millburn St. Kirkcudbright, Ph. 141.337.3877. Open April-Oct.

Galloway Sailing Centre, Loch Ken, Castle Douglas DG7 3NQ, Ph. 164.442.0626.

Mill of Fleet, Gatehouse of Fleet by the river. Open late Mar-Oct, daily 10:00am-4:30pm. Fee $.

Cream o'Galloway Dairy, Rainton Farm, Gatehouse of Fleet. Ph: 155.781.4040. Factory tours, nature trails picnic area and coffee shop.

Cardoness Castle, 1 mile SW of Gatehouse of Fleet. Open April-Sept, daily 9:30am–6:30pm, Oct-Mar, Sat and Sun 9:30am-4:30pm. Fee $.

Jean Clement's Embroidery, Ph. 155.781.4826.

Galloway Country Sports, Fordbank Country House Hotel, Bladnock, Wigtown. Speak to Jim at 198.840.2346. Lake and river fishing permits are available as are boat and tackle rentals. Salmon, brown trout, bream, roach, rudd, and perch are the local and stocked fish.

St. Ninian's Cave, At Physgill Bay, 3 miles south of Whithorn, Open daily. Free.

Whithorn Trust Discovery Centre, 45-47 George St., Whithorn. Open Apr-Oct, daily 10:30am-5pm. Fee $.

Castle Kennedy Gardens, 3 miles east of Stranraer on the A75. Open Easter-Sept, daily 10am-5pm.

Fee $. The Castle is not open to public, except for the tearoom.

<u>Northern Ireland Ferries:</u>

SeaCat, Ph. 289.032.9461. Stranraer to Belfast. This is a passenger only catamaran service.

Stena/Sealink, Ph. 289.074.7747. Stranraer to Belfast and Larne. Several sailings each day.

P&O Line, Ph. 870.242.4777. Cairnryan to Larne service is used mainly by motorists and trucks.

<u>Ardwell House Gardens</u>, Ardwell Estate, Ardwell. 10 miles south of Stranraer. Open March-Sept, daily 10am-5pm. Fee $.

<u>Logan Botanical Gardens</u>, 14 miles south of Stranraer in Port Logan. Open Mar-Oct, daily 9:30am-6pm. Fee $. Restaurant features crab and salmon salads and local produce.

<u>Mull of Galloway Nature Reserve</u>, Operated by The Royal Society for the Protection of Birds, is 4 miles south of the village of Drummore. Open daily. The information kiosk is open Tues-Sun during prime viewing mid-May to mid-July.

<u>The Southern Upland Way</u> guide is available from HMSO, 71 Lothian Road, Edinburgh EH3 9AZ.

~4~

Ayrshire –
A Breath of Fresh Ayr

The Golf Courses:

Ayr Belleisle, Ayr Seafield, Royal Troon and Turnberry

This is the land of Robert Burns and his wee beasties but that was lang, lang ago. Today the towns are vibrant and valiantly moving into a modern age. Ayrshire is more accessible than the Borders and the Galloway / Dumphries (southwest) Region towns. This accessibility is directly related to the population and the proximity of the main town, Ayr, to Glasgow - just 50 minutes away by train. Excellent train and bus service can open even the rural Ayrshire areas to those without a car.

Burns Country

For over 200 years, generations have enjoyed the poems of Robert Burns. Interest in the poetry has faded in the light of modern times but the poet has become entwined with the essence of being "Scots" and all things "Scottish". You'll find people, from Fiji to Albuquerque, raising a toast at a Burns Night Supper in commemoration of his birthday (January 25, 1759) and every New Years Eve, the world warbles *Auld Lang Syne* often not knowing Burns wrote the lyrics.

Born to an Ayrshire farmer, Burns spent nearly his whole life in Ayrshire and Dumphries and the pride and preservation of this fact can be seen throughout the cities, towns and villages of the area. The names of the preserved sites often have the names of the characters or places in his poems, so it is fun to do a little reading before you embark for Burns Country.

The towns of Kirkoswald and Alloway host Souter Johnnie's Cottage, Burns Cottage and Brig 0'Doon all featured in *Tam o'Shanter.* Mauchline offers you a chance to drink in a pub where the poet once drank himself – Poosie Nansie's Tavern. A myriad of sites are called out along the highways and byways so you can wallow in all things Burns.

Ayr

To get the lay of the land of this very active resort/port city, why not start with a pint in the <u>Tam o'Shanter</u> pub right in the heart of Ayr? Burns used this pub as the location for the poem of the same name and it still sits, in all of its ancient glory, butt-up to modern day commerce.

Ayr, the major town of the county, is bursting with energy and promise while maintaining its charm. Two rivers within the town and a long sandy beach facing the Firth of Clyde offer excellent strolls and opportunities to meet many fine canines out walking their masters.

My landlady graciously handed me Pip's leash for his morning beach stroll and I met the most fascinating Canadian woman who'd married into the town during WWII. Her boarder collie and Pip, a Jack Russell, were old diggin' buddies, so they entertained themselves while we chatted and laughed. This was a morning well spent.

Ayr has a grand shopping precinct with all the major stores represented. Restaurants abound – everything from mildly vegetarian (The Hunny Pot, 37 Beresford Terrace) to The Boathouse right on the river. I'm not sure if the Boathouse folks pay the multitude of swans to glide back and forth but I've never seen so many outside of a PBS nature show.

Ayr Racecourse is one of Britain's premier horse racing courses and offers a season that runs nearly year-round. The Scottish Grand National is held in April and what could be more exciting than placing a bet and having a go?

If you ride, there are innumerable stables that offer lessons or more adventurous fare for the experienced rider.

In May, the racecourse is home to the Ayr Show, an agricultural event very similar to American county fairs. The focus of the fair is livestock but there is also a craft fair, food court and pony trotting. The racecourse then bursts into bloom in late August (thanks to great fertilizer?) when the Ayr Flower Show takes over.

There is a professional ice hockey team (Scottish Eagles) and football team (Ayr United) in town with the usual rabid fans. I'm sure the pubs and restaurants will be full of sports widows on these evenings.

Lodging In Ayr

The dog Pip's house is on a lovely residential street that boasts a number of very nice B&Bs. I was luckily referred into The Richmond (38 Park Circus, Ayr KA7 2DL, Ph.129.226.5153) by the Tourist Information Centre on Burns Statue Square. Muir and Helen Deans made my stay extremely comfortable. Helen and I sat on the entrance hall floor and did some serious drooling over the brochures I had gotten from Turnberry. She was full of tips about places she had stayed and places she was itching to visit.

Not far from Park Circus is the Fairfield House Hotel (12 Fairfield Road, Ayr KA7 2AR, Ph. 129.226.1456). This is a 4 star hotel with what I'd call a 1930s Italianate look. The location is terrific – right at the beach with fabulous western views.

Chalmers (34 Carrick Road, Ayr KA7 2RB, Ph. & Fax 129.228.2841) will arrange to pick you up at the rail station and they have golf packages.

The Fisherton Farm Bed and Breakfast (Fisherton, Dunure, Ayr KA7 4LF, Ph. & Fax 129.250.0223) serves up a hearty dose of country life on a working farm. Convenient for Culzean Castle and Ayr.

If you are with a golfer and staying in Ayr, you are conveniently near three championship courses and many very good but not as well known links. I'd like to tell you about one of my favorite courses, Turnberry, just a little south of Ayr.

But first, before visiting Turnberry, an important stop is Culzean Castle and Park. Culzean, another castle in the chain of Clan Kennedy properties, is now overseen by the National Trust in their truly unsurpassed style. This style even trickles down to the delightful fresh flower arrangements in most of the major rooms and some tiny little blossoms in the most unexpected spots. Take a good look at these arrangements and you'll go home with a new respect for your yard's leafy shrubs and wintery twigs. It is amazing what lovely arrangements can be gleaned from what seems like a barren yard.

The entrance to Culzean is a storybook arch and bridge leading to the front door. The landscape is fairly flat at the entrance so you are totally taken aback when the house tour takes you to the sea side of the house. Here you realize the castle is sitting at the top of a vertical cliff that literally drops straight down to the rocks below. The drop and the view are breathtaking.

A unique bit of fairly modern history is that General/President Eisenhower was presented with the use of an apartment in the castle as thanks for his contribution to the British people during WWII. This was truly a thrill for him as the castle gave him a home base within driving distance of some of the world's best golf courses. I'm sure Mamie didn't complain about being left to wander this gorgeous place.

I didn't mention an oddity just off the road to Culzean. The Electric Bray is an optical illusion or so they say (Who are "they"?). I stopped at the bottom of the little hill, at the top of the hill, and just down the road for a look from a distance to see if it was real. I cannot say I saw the cars, which were going down the hill appear to go up, or vice-a-versa, but I can't say that you won't see it. Loads of people swear they've seen it over hundreds of years. I may just have been blinded by the afternoon's glorious sunshine. When you are standing at the Electric Bray look at the southern coastline for an astounding view of Culzean Castle hanging on the cliff. It does not seem real.

Turnberry

The ultimate golf widow's destination is <u>Turnberry</u> with no town in sight and no earthly need for a town. Every need or imagined need is expected and met with uncompromising service. Turnberry isn't just a golf course, but a hotel and newly added luxury spa. Come to think of it, Turnberry isn't any of those either. Turnberry (pronounced Turnbury) is an Edwardian vision of beauty and gentility that thrives in a hectic modern world.

Imagine yourself stepping down from the helicopter, thankful for your thigh high slit skirt showing off your shapely, silken legs, and then being guided inside by the doorman. You'll be greeted by the major domo, and your gown, a French ribbon satin with lace ruching, rustles in the quiet of the lobby. Magic? No, it's Turnberry.

Opened in 1906, the hotel sits high on a hill up a steeply graded drive. From the front stairs you look out onto a vista of verdant lawn drifting down to the two championship golf courses, out onto the beach, the north Irish Sea and, on a clear day, the shores of Northern Ireland. This view predominates the vast public rooms and in half of the guestrooms. For me, sitting in front of this view would be enough but when you start the Turnberry experience, you are enlivened to taste it all.

If you are a golf widow you will notice those damn clubs are nowhere to be seen: in fact you have not seen nor heard the clanking of clubs since you entered the hotel, and yet, Turnberry exists because of golf. Again it's magic! Your golfer will make his way to the seaside links, unencumbered in his new Ralph Lauren windbreaker, to find his clubs waiting for him at the first tee. And what does this mean?

Freedom!

If you must scream your delight and click your heels then take a pillow into the marble bath to muffle your joy. You must be composed and serene when you step into the royal glamour.

I'll tell you the truth, I have not stayed at Turnberry (as of yet) but I have had a facility tour with the assistant manager, Nigel Parkin. Over coffee in the Resident's Lounge, he regaled me with tales of Turnberry. We walked down long, wide hallways to view suites that looked like you could only create them in dreams. I kept pinching myself to make sure the dining room was real. The elegance was beyond words and I would swear I heard the clinking of champagne glasses and silver cutlery.

Turnberry is now a member of the Westin Hotel Group, based right in my hometown of Seattle, but Oh My God! it ain't Seattle's Westin. All life's wishes are catered to here without having to fight it out with a conventioneer from Albuquerque. You can arrange chauffeured tours, helicopter transfers, lunch with your pedicure, or hunting and fishing with a true Scots ghillie as a guide. I was extremely pleased that my hometown corporation had had the good graces to leave well enough completely alone.

Well not quite alone – a spa has been added to the Edwardian building in a very sly way. You reach the new, purpose built spa facility by an underground tunnel so that there is no skybridge or covered walkway to detract from the older building. From the outside, the spa looks like an attached farm building very similar to an oast house or the traditional Scottish distillery architecture. Inside, the light is the first thing you will notice. The windows and skylights have been placed to flood the building with as much light as possible.

The modern quest for health and beauty is very much in evidence with a workout room stocked with all manner of torturous machines and rooms where you can be worked on – massage, nails, hair, seaweed soaks and a very intriguing "pink scalp mud" treatment. If you can't bring yourself to get out of your spa robe for lunch, you are welcome to dine on healthy, chic food in the upstairs dining room. A word to the wise: don't show up for dinner in your robe as you will be shocked to find the casual looking room has been transformed for gracious dining.

I can believe that people sign up for a room in this addition and never even set foot in the hotel. I'd stay in the older building but set up camp in the spa's pool where I could float in luxury and watch the sun sink over the Irish Sea. I wonder, while drifting in the pool, if they would serve me a Manhattan with 2 cherries? Now that would be living!

Enough for dreaming away my pension. How about staying just down the road at Fairways Turnberry B&B (Fairways Lodge Road, Turnberry, KA26, 9LX, Ph. 165.533.1522, e-mail: sands.deen@virgin.net)? You'll get the same sea view and you are only a short walk from Turnberry's golf course and the hotel's lounge bar.

Prestwick and Troon

Driving north from Ayr along the coast you'll be traveling through fairly flat countryside that is just perfect for bicycling and, of course, golf. Royal Troon and Prestwick are both participating courses in the British Open Championship.

The towns along this stretch of coastline have been welcoming tourists for hundreds of years. To get the grime out of their lungs, the citizens of Glasgow migrated here for their summer holidays and they are still coming today. The towns offer up entertainment for all ages and all weather.

Prestwick International Airport was once the main airport in Scotland but it is now mainly used by charter flights.

One of the favorite activities seems to be sitting in your car along the promenade, munching your sandwich in a driving rainstorm. You won't be alone because this is Scotland and it is a day at the beach. When the rains stop, everyone wipes the crumbs away and clambers out of the car and onto the sand. This might happen several times before that sandwich is finished but who cares.

To take full advantage of the seaside you might stay with <u>Mrs. Jean MacAlister</u> (59 Beach Road, Brassie, Troon KA10 6SX, Ph. 129.231.3477) or at the <u>South Beach Hotel</u> (73 South Beach, Troon KA10 6EG, Ph. 129.231.2033, Fax 129.231.8438) which is more expensive but right next to Royal Troon.

Largs

Farther up the coast road is a fabulous resort town that is bursting with activities while still maintaining its Victorian charm. Largs has capitalized on its proximity to Glasgow and is really jumping on the weekends and all through the summer. I was here on one early March Saturday when it was cold and breezy but bright and dry. The streets were filled with the holiday crowd going into and out of the shops with ice creams and candyfloss in hand. I could imagine Victorian ladies clutching their feathered hats and children racing after hoops.

The first tourists here were Vikings and they liked it so much that they had to be forcibly evicted in 1263. Their influence on the vicinity is still in evidence. Vikingar!, the Viking Heritage Centre, explores the malingering of these visitors and in September there is a Viking Festival.

I like the sandy beach and the nice, long promenade. The seafront is lined with B&Bs and hotels. I've never stayed in Largs but I think I'd go for a room along the sea rather than back up in the town center.

You might try a cute little stone bungalow called Tigh-na-ligh Guest House (104 Brisbane Road, Largs KA30 8NN, Ph. & Fax 147.567.3975).

Kilmarnock

Not regaled in many tour books, Kilmarnock sits inland from Ayr and Troon. There are no lovely beaches to attract the summer crowds so the sad loss of industry has been especially hard felt. The overall look is of working class shabby until you realize that you are in amongst a subtle revitalization effort that may well put Kilmarnock on the map as a notable destination.

When I first drove into Kilmarnock a couple of years back, I was reminded of my first experience of Glasgow. Things were looking pretty bleak until I hit the new pedestrian mall. The paving stones have been set in a wavy pattern, and a little way up the street there are bronze, goggled swimmers coming up out of the pavement and fish leaping playfully nearby. Boy! This was a strange look amongst the shabby shops. Walking a little farther up the mall, I found a placard that told me about the underground river that actually flows beneath the street, so there is actually a reason for the wavy pavers and the swimmers bobbing up out of the waves.

A little farther along the mall, in front of Marks and Spenser, the *Bin Men Acrobats*, bronze garbage men in circus attire, serve as a good natured reminder to keep the pedestrian mall clean.

At the far end of the mall there are two bronze dogs that are looking for trouble. *Twa Dogs* are characters from the Burns poem of the same name. These two dogs, as alive today as they were 200 years ago, are polished to a high sheen from all of the children that clamber on them. The day I was there a father had to charge after his two toddlers who were hellbent to get at those dogs. Inspite of a cold rain, these little kids were hanging from, climbing on and under these perky critters that must have felt icy to the touch

Even the heartbreaking business of the local Dunblane primary school tragedy has been depicted by a kind remembrance in *Man Reading The Standard*. He sits in front of the newspaper office that had to report such sad news to the town.

Kilmarnock seems to be pulling itself up by the use of this civic art program and as you walk the town you can see the results. These works, neither formal nor old fashioned, are friendly and often humorous works that evoke a renewed civic pride.

I'm sorry, I just couldn't resist my next destination. The guide I was using gave me no description of what I would ultimately find but the name, <u>Dick Institute</u>, just made me laugh. What I found was a large civic building that had been transformed into part natural history museum, part art gallery and on that day, a traveling show of football (soccer) memorabilia. The place was packed with people and even though I really know nothing about football, American or otherwise, I enjoyed the colorful exhibit and the crowd.

The train station, a short walk from the pedestrian mall, sits beside the elevated rail line. The brick, arched rail bridge allows traffic to freely flow in and out of the town, and it gave me a reminder of the Victorian industrial revolution that made this town an important addition to the Scottish economy.

The world still treasures two of Kimarnock's products. <u>Johnnie Walker Scotch</u> and the other product, <u>Jaeger</u>, is one I have lusted after for years. The clothing design house of <u>Jaeger</u> is just outside of the town centre and still produces top quality wear for men and women. I can remember pictures in fashion magazines of Jackie Kennedy, exquisitely turned out in Jaeger slacks and ribbed turtleneck sweaters, and I always longed to look so chic. This was my chance and the prices were right.

Dean Castle, another quietly kept secret, has been restored and the grounds are now a 200 acre country park that includes all the usual amenities, plus a riding centre.

The castle has a 14th Century keep that is virtually windowless for added safety, and an adjacent 15th Century palace that contains a rich collection of tapestries, armor, and musical instruments.

Kilmarnock is not quaint, cute, or historically significant, but it is playing with the cards it has been dealt and therefore an interesting stop in what could otherwise be a fairy tale trip.

Aryshire is a pleasant country diversion with the advantage of exceptional transportation facilities. Excellent motorways will get you in and around quickly. Any one of the towns on the west coast are good bets for quick trips into Glasgow with the advantage of not having to take your car into the city. Even if you have to drive to the train station in the larger towns of Kilmarnock, Prestwick, or Ayr, you will return unharried from a full day of big city shopping and museums.

Ayrshire Diversions –

Hours & Directions

Souter Johnnie's Cottage, Main Road, Kirkoswald. 4 miles southwest of Maybole on the A77.

Open daily Easter thru Sept, 11:30am–5pm. Oct. weekends only 11:30am–5pm. Fee $.

Burns Cottage and Brig 0'Doon, Burns National Heritage Park, Murdochs Lane, Alloway. Two miles south of Ayr on the B7024.

Also includes Burns Museum, Monument, Alloway Kirk and the Tam o'Shanter Experience. Open year round.

Tam o'Shanter Experience open April-Oct 9am-6pm; Nov-Mar 9am-5pm.

Burns Cottage open April-Oct 9am-6pm; Nov-March Mon-Sat 10am-4pm, Sunday 12am-4pm. Fee $.

Poosie Nansie's Tavern, across the street from Mauchline Churchyard. Still open during regular pub hours. This is a working pub not a museum.

Tam o'Shanter, 230 Hight Street, Ayr. Open during regular pub hours.

Ayr Racecourse, Racecourse Office, 2 Whitletts Road, Ayr, Ph. 129.226.4179 for a schedule of race days.

Ayr Show, 54 East Park Road, Ayr KAB 9JQ, for details.

Ayr Flower Show, Rozelle Park, Monument Road, Ayr, Ph. 129.261.8395 or www.ayrflowershow.org.

Scottish Eagles Hockey, Centrum Arena, 123 Ayr Road, Prestwick KA9, 1TW.

Ice skating is available to the public when the ice is in place. Concerts and trade shows are also scheduled in this venue.

Ayr United, Somerset Park, Somerset Road, Ayr KA8 9NB, Ph. 129.266.3435.

Culzean Castle and Park, Maybole. 12 miles south of Ayr on the A719. Bus from Ayr.

Open April-Oct, daily 10:30am-5:30pm Fee ($$$) for both the Castle and the Park. Special events, music, and craft fairs throughout the year.

Electric Bray, on the A719, 20 miles south of Ayr. Free.

Turnberry (Turnberry Hotel, Ayrshire KA26 9LT, Ph. 165.533.1000 and Fax 165.533.1706) is on the A77 five miles north of Girvan or seventeen miles south of Ayr.

Vikingar!, The Viking Heritage Centre, Barrfields, Greenock Road, Largs. Right on the waterfront. Open 7 days a week. Fee $$.

Dick Institute, Elmbank Avenue, Kilmarnock.

Johnnie Walker Scotch. The good people here are so busy bottling and shipping that they have discontinued tours. You can still stop by and say a little prayer on this hallowed ground.

Jaeger, 15 Munro Place, Bonnyton Industrial Estate, Kilmarnock. North west of the town center. Open year round every day of the week except for the first two weeks in July when they usually close for summer holidays. There are no factory tours.

Dean Castle and Country Park, Country park open every day Dawn til Dusk and Dean Castle is open every day noon til 5pm. Fee $.

~5~

GLASGOW ~ A DEAR GREEN PLACE

The Golf Courses:

Pollock, Prestwick, Paisley, and Renfrew

I find the ancient Gaelic translation of Glasgow very amusing for my first experience of Glasgow was anything but "A Dear Green Place". Dark, dirty, rundown, violent, and football mad are the words I have always associated with Glasgow since seeing what must have been a very low point in the city's history. January 1970 and a severe windstorm had not been kind to the city which was black with centuries of accumulated soot and blacker still because of a citywide power outage. Not only were the buildings dark and morose, but the general population on the street looked down-at-the-heels, grimy and runny-nosed. I was not impressed with traveling through what seemed like endless miles of tenement slums. I was terrified that the airport bus would break down and I would reach some dreadful end in a

103

neighborhood called The Gorbals. I obviously had been reading too much Bronte.

Somewhere along the way the citizens have given themselves a good shake and a pep talk because a massive dose of civic pride was needed to rise up out of the soot and pollution to win the 1990 European City of Culture Award. This award had been previously won by the likes of Athens, Paris, and Berlin. With this new found pride the city moved on to win the U.K. City of Architecture and Design Award in 1999.

Now the third largest city in Britain, Glasgow is the vibrant economic heart of Scotland. A full one third of Scotland's population lives in and around the city which has discovered that if you scrape off the soot, you'll find really lovely, honey and rust colored stone buildings. Even once beleaguered tenements stand proudly beside the former residences of extravagant tobacco barons and shipping magnates.

Today, Victorian buildings in the heart of the business district are being renovated at a clip close to the speed of sound. Many of the huge limestone, sandstone, brick, and granite buildings stand empty, just waiting to be turned into affordable apartments, posh condos, or trendy businesses with stylish, exclusive shops on their ground floors.

Modern architecture is being thoughtfully integrated into the landscape with many traditional Glasgow signatures being incorporated into the designs. I think it is now time to introduce one of the design practitioners of what has become known as "Glasgow Style".

Charles Rennie MacKintosh

Born in 1868, the 11th child of a Glasgow policeman, Charles Rennie Mackintosh apprenticed himself with an architectural firm while also attending the Glasgow School of Art. Mackintosh and three school chums started working in the "Glasgow Style" a highly stylized form of art nouveau that was all the rage on The Continent. "The Four," as they became known, worked closely on all aspects of a design project. Mackintosh eventually married one of "The Four", Margaret Macdonald, and they gained international repute in Europe, but Scotland had not yet discovered "Mackintosh" design.

After entering and winning a design competition for the new Glasgow School of Art in 1896, Mackintosh, like his American contemporary, Frank Lloyd Wright, started to attract the attention of forward thinking, wealthy patrons with his innovative designs, but he remained relatively unknown to the general population of Scotland.

Today in design circles worldwide the name "Mackintosh" connotes a style that has overshadowed the older "Glasgow Style". Chairs designed by Charles in

1900 are still in production, and Margaret's sensuous rose motif adorns china, jewelry, and fabric. The Mackintosh Society has made strenuous efforts to maintain the integrity and quality of products produced using the Mackintoshes' designs and is actively involved in the preservation of Charles Rennie Mackintosh's architectural work.

The Mackintosh House, on the campus of Glasgow University, though not the original house, contains the original house's contents arranged as if they had been placed by Mackintosh himself. If you are familiar with Frank Lloyd Wright's work, you will be astonished at the similarities in the furniture.

In the wide pedestrian shopping precinct of Sauchiehall Street, you can have lunch in The Willow Tearooms, just as ladies dined in 1904, surrounded by Margaret's stained glass, Charles' chairs and light fixtures. Miss Kate Cranston, a local entrepreneur, recognized Charles' unique talent and commissioned him to design several tearooms. The Sauchiehall Street outlet has survived nearly intact. This is a perfect spot for a morning coffee or a late afternoon snack but the lunch menu appeared to be unchanged since 1904 - edible but uninspired.

Now that you are armed with a new arsenal of design motifs, you can venture out into the city and spot them everywhere.

Public transportation is excellent in Glasgow. The train stations and bus stations are all within the main shopping district and the underground is clean and safe. Local in-city busses and taxis abound, so you can stay anywhere in or around Glasgow.

Driving is another matter altogether. One way streets, dead ends and the curious habit of having a street name change, sometimes block by block, makes driving a daunting proposition. Another unusual phenomenon is the casual way squares are numbered - sometimes clockwise and then again, maybe counterclockwise. By adding in the looming, flat facades and lack of clearly visible signage and happily, or unhappily if you prefer, I got the lay of the land by driving aimlessly around and around. I eventually settled for the first hotel that came into sight, with a parking garage nearby. I parked that car and left it for the duration of my stay. I can now confidently get back to the street of B&Bs that I discovered on my next day's walk. Why hadn't I seen them while I was dodging traffic and following a delivery van?

Lodging In Glasgow

It really doesn't matter what time of the year one arrives in Glasgow because rooms are at a premium. Unlike Edinburgh, the prime tourist town of Scotland, there are not blocks and blocks of guesthouses and hotels, so booking your room in advance is a necessity. You might wonder why I didn't have a room booked in advance. Well if you remember my admonition on using the internet for booking in the "Hints and Horrors" chapter, then you'll know I hit a snag. I tried e-mailing a half dozen establishments and got not one response, even though they were prominently advertised on the Scottish Tourist Board list. Reserve early, use the fax number if you have no e-mail response, or if all else fails, phone your place of choice.

So where did I end up staying? The Holiday Inn Express. Hey! I told you the traffic was horrible and I had had it and ... oh shut up.

The Holiday Inn Express (165 West Nile Street, Glasgow G1 2RL, Ph. 141.331.6800, Fax 141.331.6828) is a business person's Holiday Inn and right next door to the upscale Holiday Inn (161 West Nile Street, Ph. 141.332. 0110). The Express is not plush but the self-service breakfast that came with the room, the hot shower, and the location were fabulous. I looked right out at the Glasgow Royal Concert Hall and the start of the Buchanan Street shopping precinct.

The Rennie Mackintosh Hotel (218-220 Renfrew Street, Ph. 141.333.9992) is just to the west of the Glasgow School of Art on a quiet street. The hotel is small and decorated in the Mackintosh style. If they are booked I'm sure they will be able to find you a room at one of the other small hotels on their block.

Shopping In Glasgow

A young English friend just loves to nip up to Glasgow for what she calls "brilliant" shopping. Huge new American style malls like the <u>Buchanan Galleries</u> have joined the old and traditional like the <u>Argyll Arcade</u>. <u>Princess Square</u> is a great visual treat because the old and new come together under an updated Victorian glass arcade roof. The pedestrian only shopping streets, Buchanan, Sauchiehall, and Argyll, boast the best, worst, hippest and the stodgiest in British ashion. They also offer the world to the Glaswegians. Shops that grace American malls are in evidence here as are French, Italian, Scandinavian, African, and Asian.

The <u>Trongate</u>, a once derelict warehouse district, has been discovered by young executive types. Dour facades now sport steel and glass additions on the roof and out back. A new gentility has found its way into the heart of the city and smug urbanites walk to work instead of suffering gridlock, expensive parking, and stop-and-go rush hour traffic on the motorway.

The <u>Old Fruitmarket</u>, at the heart of the Trongate area, is now a warren of pubs and restaurants and regularly hosts special events including the <u>Glasgow International Jazz Festival</u>.

Scotland's largest indoor market, <u>The Barras</u> (the barrows or pushcarts), is a little hike down Trongate to Gallowgate but this tatty and rundown market may offer you the chance for some real treasure hunting. It is like a permanent, indoor garage sale. This neighborhood has yet to see much renovation so don't expect trendy eateries and shops.

Musems of Note in Glasgow

The hardworking citizens of a depressingly crowded city (once the second largest city in Britain after London) found respite in its municipal museums. Long hours and horrid conditions were what most people dealt with daily, so a trip to a stately building to experience beautiful, interesting, and exotic objects must have been a welcomed relief. The noble, wealthy city fathers who employed these overworked minions, were kind enough to make the admission to the city's museums free and today they are still free, though contributions are encouraged.

Kelvingrove Art Gallery & Museum opened in 1888 for a Grand Exhibition where Queen Victoria must have felt right at home. This ornate, red sandstone building, located in Kelvingrove Park, offers a bit of everything from stuffed critters to a surprising number of French Impressionist paintings. The fine art collection alone contains more than 3,000 oils and 12,500 drawings, etchings, and prints. The day I visited there was an exciting international photography exhibit of animal wildlife.

While you are out in the West End why not wander through the gardens of Kelvingrove Park and up the hill to Glasgow University (founded in 1451) and its wealth of museums. The <u>University Visitors Center</u> offers tours but call first to find out about the times, as they vary.

The <u>Hunterian Art Gallery</u> has a fabulous collection of American artist James MacNeill Whistler's work besides Pisarro, Rembrandt and Rodin.

The <u>Hunterian Museum</u> has really, really, old stuff. How about dinosaur eggs or death masks or ethnological oddities?

The <u>MacKintosh House</u> is on campus too. Get a look at household items of one of the most influential design innovators of relatively modern times.

Some of the other museums within the city are:

The <u>Gallery of Modern Art</u>, a staid, old columned building behind a statue of Lord Wellington, will give you the impression that nothing fun has ever happened here. Walk around to the back of the building and you'll find the back wall has been replaced with glass. Through these windows you can see that a great deal of fun is being had and you will be seduced inside.

In the evenings you may stroll past the classical statue of Lord Wellington and discover he is wearing an orange traffic cone. The local rowdies cannot be dissuaded from this practice. Every workday morning a municipal worker takes the cone off and Wellington is back to his dour self.

<u>St. Mungo Museum of Religious Life and Art</u>. A new facility (1993) showcases the art of the world's

religions. The collection is vast and sometimes controversial. Don't miss the tearoom that opens onto a Zen Garden or a stroll through the Necropolis, an elaborate cemetery, next door.

The Tenement House. Once upon a time a very old lady lived as she always had lived. When that nice old lady died, she left a living museum of life in the 19th Century. Nothing had been changed, not even the gas lamps or the primitive bathing facilities, and now the National Trust for Scotland lovingly maintains this tiny apartment.

Museum of Transport. Ever dreamed of owning a fine Scottish-made Arrol-Johnston? "A what?" you say. A car or more properly a motorcar, of distinction if not longevity, can be seen here with other fine modes of transportation ranging from horse drawn trams to steam trains.

Taking a jaunt out of the downtown proper can open a whole different venue of museums and one of my all time favorites:

The Burrell Collection

Do you have a collection of salt and peppers or little silver baby cups? I have a demitasse spoon collection that seldom grows unless I'm in a new foreign country. But what if you were overrun by a collection as my college roommate has become. The black and white cow rules her life and her long list of friends have not helped her with this affliction. I love looking for little ceramic cows, yard ornament cows, cow skirts and black and white spotted bathroom towels that will fit in with the whole house décor. If you can relate to a collection, you'll love what has now been named <u>The Burrell Collection</u>.

Young William Burrell was sent out with 10 shillings in his pocket to buy himself a cricket bat. He came home with a painting. I'm sure Dad was ticked but William was tickled with his find and hooked on finding his next treasure.

Over the next 80 plus years, William became a wealthy shipping magnate and collected in earnest. He catalogued every purchase, large or small, in a school notebook. Sir William meticulously kept detailed item notes and prices. In 1944 Sir William and his wife, Lady Constance, gave the collection to the City of Glasgow with a few troublesome stipulations. He required a new museum to be built for the whole collection, not less than 16 miles from the Royal Exchange in downtown Glasgow and within 4 miles of the town of Killearn, now a suburb of Glasgow. Even in 1944, Sir William realized that the pollution generated by the industries in Glasgow, some of which he owned, was harmful to his ancient sculpture and paintings, so he wanted a rural, pristine setting for his treasures.

The City of Glasgow, struggling with post war problems, shipyard closures, and decaying neighborhoods was hard pressed to come up with the money, so the 4,000 piece collection was packed in crates and stored whereever space could be found. A committee was formed to devise a plan because if they couldn't build a museum then the cross country rival Edinburgh would get the collection. Time passed.

Sir William Burrell collected until the day he died in 1957. The collection by then was at 8,000 pieces and the committee was still bickering and scheming. The new crates were piled on top of the old and the problem grew.

Luckily property was donated from the grounds of <u>Pollock House and Pollock Country Park</u> and a design competition was announced in 1971. Even the competition was a trial, as Sir William had salvaged impressive architectural pieces and they would have to be incorporated into the actual building. Which crate were they in and where was that crate?

In 1983, the first visitors passed through the front door, an arched, castle gate from Hornby Castle in Yorkshire, and they were swept up by the varied scope of The Burrell Collection.

Sir William collected what he liked or what caught his eye. Full rooms from Hutton Castle, the Burrell's estate, have been installed. A huge Grecian urn dominates one room, while in a long gallery that looks out onto a woodland vista, there are displays of everything from ancient Chinese pottery, Italian paintings, to gossamer, handmade lace panels. God only knows what's still in crates in the basement.

Easily reached by taxi, bus, or train from downtown Glasgow, a day at The Burrell Collection and Pollock House's splendid collection of Spanish paintings is time well spent. There is literally something for everyone but don't expect to see a cricket bat.

The museum has a wonderful greenhouse windowed café that is hung with medieval stained glass. You can eat inside or take a picnic out into the country park and dangle your feet in White Cart Water. An added attraction, if you are with a golfer, is the Pollock Golf Course right next door.

Eating Out and Evenings Out In Glasgow

Glasgow's downtown is filled with great places to eat and the places are busy. If you are walking during the day and see a place you'd like to try for dinner, then pop in and reserve a table right then and there. I got a great recommendation for an Italian place from the girl at the hotel's front desk, but I was turned out into a chilly night by a maitre'd who looked frazzled because of the crowd waiting in the lobby. I ended up in a place around the corner that wasn't much to look at but the pizza was great, and my very entertaining waiter sat down with me during his break. I did notice, after taking my seat in the front of the restaurant, that there was a back dining room that offered more ambience but probably not the friendly waiter.

On my walk back from the Kelvingrove Art Museum, I passed Irish, Chinese, Indian, and even a

Mexican place and all of them seemed to be jumping. I had a great meal in a pub/restaurant called Waxy O'Connor's (46 West George St.). The menu was fun. Where else could I have had to choose between Haggis Neeps and Tatties (with whisky gravy), Warm Duck Salad, Lamb Steak with Ratatouille, and Wild Scottish Smoked Salmon Sandwich? The business-attired crowd was lively and appeared to have come straight from work for an evening of beer, laughs, and live music.

Not far from Waxy O'Connors is Rogano (11 Exchange Place), a splendid old art deco fish house. It reminded me a lot of San Francisco fish houses. The Oyster Bar upstairs is pricey for dinner but can be a bargain at lunch. The café downstairs is good at all times.

For a little livelier venue try The Piper's Tryst in the National Museum of Piping (30-34 McPhater St) where you will hear continuous pipe music and be able to sample traditional rumbledethumps. The everyday crowd is probably pretty fun too because the pub is right across the street from Scottish Television.

Two pubs located on the Clyde Walkway that look less than tantalizing, in fact they look like dumps, host some of the best Scottish folk music in the country. Clutha Vaults (167 Stockwell Street) and Victoria Bar (157-59 Bridgegate) will offer a warm welcome and surprisingly nice interiors.

I must admit that the night I went by the Drum and Monkey (93-95 St. Vincent's Street), the huge

Victorian bar was filled to overflowing and I just couldn't see fighting my way to the bar for a drink. The crowd looked like okay young folks though.

A word of warning if you are feeling like a cheap fish and chips meal and you stumble across the Ubiquitous Chip (12 Ashton Lane, off Byres Rd) remember this Michelin rated restaurant serves spectacular bistro style food with Scottish overtones. The restaurant has a 2-course, price fixed lunch for $32.00 and dinner goes on up from there. Bar meals range from about $13 at lunch to $25.00 at dinner. Not your cheap fish and chips but splurge worthy.

For a real bargain try any street corner fish and chips shop. Many now sell chicken and pizza too.

If you are looking for an evening filled with more than beer, wine, and song, just remember that Glasgow has won the European City of Culture Award and that involves much more than piping and folksongs.

World-class homegrown and international talent can be seen at the following venues and many others around the city. Do some early homework so as not to be disappointed. These events are often "Sold Out" early because Glaswegians take their culture very seriously.

The Theatre Royal is the home of Scottish Opera and Scottish Ballet. Jazz, musicals, and theatrical productions are also booked in here.

Glasgow Royal Concert Hall is the home of the Royal Scottish National Orchestra. The Concert Hall also hosts an International Series with visiting artists, the Scottish Fiddle Orchestra, children's concerts and holiday galas throughout the year.

The Tron Theatre stages contemporary Scottish and international performances and houses the excellent Café at the Tron and the Victorian Bar and Restaurant.

Perhaps Scotland's premier theatre is the Citizens' Theatre that produces *au courant* plays with political themes.

If you are in for a "real" Glasgow experience then you might want to get football tickets. The Celtics and the Rangers are the two professional hometown teams and they draw huge crowds of drunken fans. I know this sounds like I'm generalizing but if only half of the 60,000 fans are drunk, that's still a ton of drunks. Be prepared to be overwhelmed by the noise, don't dress up, wear sensible shoes, and as in any crowd, keep your purse safe.

If you have survived the football or decided to pass on it entirely, then how about a cruise on the *Waverley*, the last seagoing paddle steamer in the world? She chugs down the River Clyde and makes several stops along the way.

As you glide down the river take a look at the Clyde Centre, a sleek aluminum conference center, that snugs up against the River Clyde looking very much like its nickname, "The Armadillo".

Day Trips Out Of Glasgow

New Lanark, World Heritage Village

New Lanark is literally a new town, founded in 1785 by the Glasgow industrialist David Dale and managed by his son-in-law, Robert Owen. They set about a bold experiment concerning the working and living conditions of their mill workers. The town encompassed one of largest cotton mills in the world and it included mills, stores and housing for the workers. The mill was powered by the water of the Falls of Clyde. At its height, the town had a population of 2,000.

Owen felt that if the workers were in healthy surroundings and treated well, they would work harder for the mill. These were revolutionary thoughts for the time. Children under the age of 10 were not allowed to work in the mills and music and dancing were taught to the workers.

The mills were in production until 1968, and shortly thereafter, the restoration of the site began. In 1986 the site was nominated to the World Heritage Site list. Today the mill complex is intact and supports museums in the Village Store, Mill Workers' House, and Robert Owen's House. There are craft workshops, coffee shops, restaurants and a wild life centre. The Visitor Centre features the Annie MacLeod Experience, a look at 1820 mill life through the eyes of a ten year old girl.

The Mill Hotel and Waterhouses (Ph. 155.566.7200, Fax 155.566.7222) and also a youth hostel allow you to stay in the village that still has a small permanent population living in the old mill worker's houses.

Train Daytrips

Glasgow's excellent train and bus system allows for day trips to the surrounding countryside without the need for a car. You can spend a day at the beach in Ayr, see the Paisley Shawl Museum, or visit Stirling Castle. If you plan it right, you can get a train at 9:30am, ride as far as Aberdeen, have a full afternoon's poke around and be back in your hotel in Glasgow before 11pm. Now that's what I call packing in the fun.

Glasgow Diversions –

Hours & Directions

Glasgow School of Art, 167 Renfrew Street, Glasgow. Tours are available Mon-Fri 11am and 2pm, Sat 10:30am and 11:30am. During July and Aug additional tours are added Sat 1pm, and Sun. 10:30am, 11:30am and 1pm. Fee $$.

The Mackintosh Society, Queen's Cross Church, 870 Garscube Road, Glasgow G20 7EL. The Society offices are within Queen's Cross Church the only church designed by Mackintosh and built. Open year round Mon

– Fri 10am–5pm, Sat 10am-2pm and Sun 2pm-5pm. Donations welcomed.

Mackintosh House, University of Glasgow, Hillhead Street, Glasgow. Open year round Mon–Sat 9:30am–5pm Closed for lunch 12:30pm–1:30pm. Free.

The Willow Tearooms, 217 Sauchiehall Street, Glasgow. Open year round Mon – Sat 9:30-4:30, Sun 12-4:15. This is a working and very popular restaurant.

Buchanan Galleries Several blocks worth of shops at the top of Buchanan Street, next to the Glasgow Royal Concert Hall. Open regular shop hours with some late evening hours as well.

Argyll Arcade – Located at the bottom of the Buchanan Street Pedestrian Mall near the intersection with Argyll Street. Open regular shop hours. Smaller shops may not cater to late evening shopping. Some very nice jewelry shops here in all price ranges.

Princess Square – Located midway on the Buchanan Street Pedestrian Mall. Open regular shop hours with some late evening hours as well. Some of the restaurants are accessible for late night dining.

Trongate – Walk east on Argyll Street and the street becomes Trongate. Many of the cities' old civic buildings are in the northern section of this area. These glorious old civic buildings are cuddled up to modern shops, warehouses cum condos and lively eateries.

Old Fruitmarket is located at Bell and Albion. This area supports a huge number of pubs and restaurants.

Glasgow International Jazz Festival, Ph. 141.287.5511. The Festival usually runs the last week of June and the first week of July.

The Barras – Just off Gallowgate on Rose and Kent Streets. Open every day but busiest on weekends.

Kelvingrove Art Gallery & Museum, Kelvingrove Park in the West End. Mon-Sat 10am–5pm and Sun. 11am–5pm. Free.

Glasgow University and University Visitors Center, University Avenue. Open Oct-April, Mon-Sat 9:30am–5pm; May-Sept also Sunday 2pm–5pm. Free. Guided tours charge a fee.

Hunterian Art Gallery, University of Glasgow, Hillhead St. Mon-Sat 9:30am-5pm. Free.

Hunterian Museum, University of Glasgow, Gilmorehill Building. Open Mon–Sat 9:30am–5pm. Free.

Mackintosh House, next door to the Hunterian Art Museum. Open Mon-Sat 9:30am–5pm. Free.

Gallery of Modern Art - located in Royal Exchange Square at the junction of Ingram and Queen streets. Free.

St. Mungo Museum of Religious Life and Art located on Cathedral Square just off Castle Street. Open year round Mon-Sat 10am–5pm and Sun 11am–5pm.

Shares space with the Royal Infirmary and Glasgow Cathedral. All of them are Free.

Tenement House, 145 Beccleuch Street, Glasgow. Very near the Glasgow Art School. Open daily Mar–Oct, 2pm-5pm. Fee $$.

Museum of Transport, Kelvin Hall, 1 Bunhouse Road, Glasgow. Located in the west end of Glasgow. Open all year, Mon-Thurs and Sat 10am–5pm, Fri and Sun 11am-5pm. Free.

The Burrell Collection, Pollok Country Park, 2060 Pollokshaws Road, Glasgow. The subway and the bus (57 or 57A from downtown) will get you close to the park gates and a park bus runs every hour, on the half hour, from the front entrance to the Burrell. Open all year, Mon-Thur and Sat 10am-5pm, Fri and Sun 11am-5pm. Free.

Pollock House, just across the road from The Burrell. Open daily April-Oct 10am-5pm; Nov-Mar 11am-4pm. Fee $$. The family seat of the Maxwell Clan. Tearoom.

The Theatre Royal, Hope Street, Ph.141.322.3321.

Glasgow Royal Concert Hall, 2 Sauchiehall Street, Ph.141.353.4137, Website: www.grch.com.

The Tron Theatre, 63 Trongate, Ph. 141.552.4267.

Citizens' Theatre, 119 Gorbals Street, Glasgow, Ph. 141.429.0022.

Celtic Football Club plays on the east side of Glasgow at Parkland, Ph. 141.552.8591.

Rangers Football Club plays on the west side of Glasgow at Ibrox, Ph. 141.427.8500. Footballers do actually eat and you might try Argyle House Restaurant overlooking the turf.

Waverley, Anderston Quay, Glasgow, Ph. 141.221.8152. Call or ask the Tourist Office for a current schedule. The boat splits time between Ayr and Glasgow. Fee $$$.

Clyde Centre, far west end of Anderston Quay. You'll see it. It looks like a stainless steel armadillo.

New Lanark, about an hour outside of Glasgow off the M74. Visitor Center, Ph.155.566.1345 or visit the web site at www.newlanark.org or e-mail visit@newlanark.org. Open year round. Fee $$.

-6-

The Western Highlands and Islands

The Golf Courses:

Ft. Willaim, Isle of Skye Golf Club, Lochcarron, Macrihanish and Maillaig.

Just above Glasgow and to the west, you will be in the most rugged countryside in all of Scotland. There is no easy way to get anywhere here because of the surprising terrain you encounter around every bend in the road. Delicate fingers of the North Atlantic pierce the coastline, sturdy fingers of land jut out into the sea, forested mountains rise up, and long thin lakes lay at the bottom of ancient glens, and each of these seems to fall directly in your line of travel. Driving here will involve seeing a lot of the road you will be traveling or the one you have just traveled - just over there across the loch or valley. But that is what makes this part of Scotland so stunningly beautiful.

You won't travel fast between points but the two lane roads are very good and there usually isn't much traffic unless you take the road to Loch Lomond on a summer weekend.

Towns and villages are few and far between and that means train service is less than terrific, though there is good service to Oban and Fort William. If you are driving, watch your gas tank because you won't find a pump behind every tree.

In fact, you won't find a gas pump behind every castle either because many of the castles in this region back right up to the water. Sometimes they are on small islands just a stone's throw from the shore. These castles, or small fortresses, were built on the water for ease of transportation, delivery of goods and quick getaway from the army coming down the glen. Unfortunately the Danes could row right up to the back door but that's another story. Many of the smaller island castles are ruined and unapproachable but make terrific photo stops. One of my little favorites just sits there looking cute without even a mention on the map. When it appears, I'm not sure if I am dreaming or not.

Golf Courses, if needed, are also fewer and farther between than even the towns. You should be able to find a course in many of the larger towns and for sure in Oban and Ft. William.

I have two favorite ways of getting to this region from Glasgow. I'll start with my very favorite.

Drive west out of Glasgow to the old ship building city of Gourock, and take the ferry across the River Clyde to the little resort town of Dunoon. This is the most striking route because you sail from a heavily industrial city right into a Highland port.

The second route is up through the heavily populated suburbs of Glasgow to the banks of Loch Lomond. Once you reach the loch, you are treated to gentle hills and a huge lake studded with small islands. You can stop in Balloch at the south end of the lake and take a cruise with Sweeney's Cruisers that will leave your heart singing *Loch Lomond*. The only drawback to this route is that the lake is only 20 miles from Glasgow. The road can be gridlocked on summer weekends when it seems every Glaswegian has come to enjoy the lake.

Using either route, the first stop should be Inveraray the ancestral home of the Dukes of Argyll (not even similar to the Dukes of Hazard) and the seat of the Clan Campbell. This is Campbell country and if you have a connection to the clan, you may want to spend time wandering the landscape here and about.

Inveraray Castle reminds me of a German fairytale castle or a French chateau with a turret at each corner. The family is in residence and they offer tours of the house. If you are a gardener, you can make prior arrangements to tour the extensive grounds.

The teensy little town of Inveraray has several hotels but the one of most interest, if you like to cook, is

Creggan's Inn (Strachur PA27 8BX, Ph. 136.986.0279). Sir Charles MacLean and his mother run the inn and its world class restaurant. They are open for lunch and dinner, and reservations are a must. After tasting venison, lamb, Aberdeen Angus, and straight from the sea delights, you can purchase Lady MacLean's best-selling cookbooks in the gift shop.

Disreputable visitors have spent time in the Inveraray Jail but the accommodations were less than cushy. Now voted *Best Scottish Attraction of the Decade*, you can visit the medieval punishment exhibit, try the whipping table, and listen to trials in the 1820 courtroom. The guides are dressed in costume to make the experience more true to life.

If you are not going to have time to poke around on the Mull of Kintyre and want to get to Oban post haste, or as soon as the roads will let you, then take the squiggly red line on your map marked A819. You'll come out at Kilchurn Castle on Loch Awe and the views are awesome.

Oban

Known as the Capital of the Western Highlands, Oban is a very lively town indeed. You'll feel the excitement of a place that depends on the weather and good sailing to keep it going. The rail line comes right down to the docks for easy access to the southern

Hebredies ferries. Once a very busy fishing port, Oban now serves the islands with goods, services, and tourists. There are hotels and guest houses lined up around the harbor and restaurants that help to feed the hordes. The town has a lively schedule of entertainments that attract townfolk and farmers from great distances. There is a large Highland Games in August, music festivals and theatre throughout the year. Look for flyers in shop windows to see if you need to tear yourself away from the pub for a local charity benefit or a famous name who has been lured to the hinterland by curiosity.

Right by the docks you can tour the <u>Oban Distillery</u>, eat a Chinese meal, or shop for bargains at the <u>Caithness Glass Company Factory Shop</u>. If there is a visible sunset predicted, take the climb up to <u>McCaig's Tower</u>, a folly that looks like the Roman Coliseum, for a view out over the Southern Hebriedes. Take your evening hors d' oeuvre along, stake out a bench, and relax into a pre-dinner reverie.

The surrounding countryside supports various attractions including the <u>Oban Rare Breed Farm</u>, and the <u>Oban Seal and Marine Centre</u>.

The islands of <u>Mull</u>, <u>Lynn of Lorne</u>, <u>Coll</u> and <u>Tiree</u> have ferry service from Oban and day trips can be arranged. These islands are sparsely populated and should be researched and your room reserved before you go across for an overnight or extended stay.

Lodging In Oban

Kilchrenan House (Corran Esplanade, Oban PA34 5QA, Ph. 163.156.2663) is a large Victorian guesthouse right on the sea front.

Drumriggend (Mrs. Elaine Robertson, Pulpit Hill, Oban PA34 4LX, Ph. 163.156.2840), a small private home in 4 acres of garden, sits high above the harbor and has unobstructed views to the islands.

Glencoe

Once again the road will follow the shoreline of Loch Linnhe almost all the way to Fort William. About half way you'll come to a sign pointing you to the town of Glencoe, where in 1692 the MacDonald Clan was hosting the Campbell Clan, their sworn enemies, to shelter during a winter coldsnap. The treacherous Campbells betrayed the hospitality, and on the order of England's King William III, massacred 40 MacDonalds for their failure to sign an oath of loyalty to the King. This was a very dark day for the MacDonalds and they still look on the Campbells with suspicion.

Today, the National Trust of Scotland runs the informative Visitor Centre at Glencoe and there are also excellent skiing, hiking and climbing facilities in the glen. The Glencoe Ski Centre keeps the lifts open all summer to get you right up into the hills. Keep an eye out for red deer, wild cats and golden eagles.

Fort William

Whether arriving by train, bus, or car, we're here in a straight-laced town with a great supermarket. That doesn't sound very nice but it seems like I'm always in need of more "car food" when I get to Fort William, and I head right for the supermarket just off the main carpark and right by the train station.

The town itself offers a great shopping street and attracts holiday-makers and, like Oban, people from miles around. The next large shopping spot is Inverness, just 65 miles of tourist and truck clogged, 2 laned road away.

Fort William was at the heart of the Highland Clearances when tenant farmers were thrown off the land in favor of huge sheep farms. Many American and Canadian families of Scots descent may have ties to this port. Make a stop at the West Highland Museum for an outstanding collection of items from the time of the Clearances.

Ben Nevis (4,406 feet) is Britain's highest peak and if you are fit enough and are prepared with heavy duty hiking gear, you'll find the eight hour round trip for the superlative view worth the effort. Remember, this is a mountain and the weather can change rapidly so be prepared.

If you haven't come prepared but are sorely tempted to try the trails, then Ben Nevis Woollen Mill has the outdoor gear you'll need besides the traditional woollen mill fare.

If you are truly a climbing diehard, then try the Ben Nevis Race. You too can run up the mountain with 500 other fools for the honor, the MacFarland Cup, and a £50 note.

Lodging In Fort William

Queen Victoria visited Fort William in 1870 and stayed in the newly completed mansion of Baron Abinger. You can feel like a queen and stay in that same mansion now called Inverlochy Castle (Torlundy, Fort William PH33 6SN, Ph. 139.770.2177). You will be pampered in the lap of luxury surrounded by antiques, artwork and fresh cut flowers. Another budget blower, but it caused a queen to say "I never saw a lovelier or more romantic spot."

I've never stayed in Fort William, as I much prefer staying right on the sea front in Oban, but there are plenty of B&B and guest houses to meet any requirements.

The Great Glen

Leaving Fort William on the A82 you will enter The Great Glen, an ancient fault line that filled with water forming a series of lakes, including Loch Ness. In 1822 the Caledonian Canal joined the lakes (lochs) with 29 locks, and now water traffic and maybe the Loch Ness Monster can easily cross the country from Atlantic to the North Sea.

The A82, the only direct road to Inverness, is extremely scenic. It follows the lakes' shorelines nearly the whole way. With no alternate route you will find lots of traffic. Many of the motorists are hoping for a "Nessie" sighting so they aren't always aware of the traffic congestion they are causing. Just take a deep breath and enjoy the scenery.

A fabulous photo stop, as you near Inverness, is Urquhart Castle. The ruin sits high above the waters of Loch Ness and sunset shots here are spectacular. Most of the "Nessie" sightings have been made from this location so make sure you have extra film.

If you have driven as far as Fort William or you drove straight north to Inverness from Edinburgh, then you are ready for a real driving adventure.

Half way down The Great Glen, at a spot called Invergarry, take the A87 to Kyle of Lochalsh which is little more than a hotel and a railway station (from

Inverness). The real attraction is the bridge to the Isle of Skye and its desolate, treeless beauty.

Along the A87 you'll come to much photographed Eilean Donan Castle. If you watch PBS Television, you'll be familiar with the image of this place. The BBC uses a shot of the castle with a hot air balloon to announce that they have produced the program you are about to watch. Eilean Donan was built in 1214 on a small island to fend off the Danes. Colonel MacRae of Clan MacRae brought the castle back from 200 years of neglect and it is now a showplace of Clan MacRae related items. There is also a scenic little causeway so you can easily walk out to the castle.

Kyle of Lochalsh, the end of the line for the railway, used to be the place where you arrived and hoped the weather was good enough for the ferry to be running to Skye. Kyle of Lochalsh still isn't much more than a couple of hotels, but there are no long waits for the weather as the new bridge will take you over the sea to Skye in a matter of minutes and for a hefty toll.

Isle of Skye

Skye is not for the person who is already suffering from urban withdrawal. Skye is a magical place of mists, and moors, and craggy mountains, and these are all packed into a island not more than 25 miles at its widest and 48 miles long. There are very few people here, and those that do live here are hardy and devoted to the island. They stay because of the exquisite natural beauty and maybe a fairy curse or two. About 60% of Skye's population speaks Scots Gaelic and the island boasts the only Gaelic college in all of Scotland.

The Vikings settled in about 860AD and there are still Norse place names scattered around the island. The Scots have been firmly in command of Skye since 1263. The Skye Museum of Island Life, housed in several thatched cottages, is an excellent facility with exhibits showing the evolution of Scots life here.

Contrary to their practical traits the Scots have never been capable of passing up a good legend. Haggisland in Portree is a perfect example of a legend gone awry, but at Dunvegan Castle, the seat of Clan MacLeod, you'll see The Fairy Flag, a gift from the fairy wife of the 4th Chief of the Clan, is still on display in the castle. The MacDonalds are less fortunate because of their enviable power. Most all of the MacDonald castles now stand in ruin. The Clan Donald Center, near the ruin of Armadale Castle, is in a renovated gardener's cottage called Armadale House.

Lord and Lady MacDonald live in Kinloch Lodge (Isleornsay, Sleat, Isle of Skye IV43 8QY, Ph. 01471 833333), a white stone hunting lodge built in 1680. The lodge, on the Sleat Peninsula, is not just their private home but a first rate hotel as well. Lady MacDonald has written numerous cookbooks and her cooking style imaginatively uses the produce of the Hebrides. This is a special treat of a place.

The island does have a small golf course. The Isle of Skye Golf Club has nine holes and a guy who runs the snack bar and cuts the grass as needed.

Like Seattle, the weather is grey, drizzly, and damp for most of the year. What do the islanders do with their time? They knit, paint, pot, carve, play music, make jewelry and weave. There are many local crafts shops and even cottages where the resident's product is displayed by the road. You'll love ferreting out the perfect souvenir or gift on Skye.

Speaking of ferrets, you may be interested in the Skye Serpentarium. The kind (and, I think, kinda weird) folks here breed, and rescue snakes, lizards, turtles, and frogs. You can even buy baby snakes. I'll stick with the trusty ferret.

From Skye, you can ferry to many of the other Heberdian Islands for even more unusual discoveries. The island of Harris makes tweed and Lewis... well, I'm not sure about Lewis. The MacLeod's of Lewis weren't too discerning about color choices in their tartan so I'm sort of leery of Lewis. Of course I haven't been there and it may actually be absolutely fabulous.

Whether or not you made it to Skye, you have a decision to make on your route of travel away from Kyle of Lochalsh. You can hie thyself back down the road you came on and head for Inverness on the Loch Ness road, or take the northerly route over the desolate moors and drop down into Inverness from the north. Depending on your available time, this whole route, from Fort William to Lochalsh, then to Lochcarron and on to Inverness, can be done in a long day.

I would like to recommend that you spend a night in the little village of Lochcarron, to the north of Lochalsh. The main street looks out onto the loch and the hills of Attadale. This is a true Highland village with one exception. There is a small golf course here, where as most wee towns and villages don't have one.

There is one hotel, the Rockavilla, (Main Street, Lochcarron, Ph. 152.072.2379) and several B&Bs in and around the town. The hotel offers fresh scallops on the menu, which have been caught by the proprietor of the hotel himself.

Just to the south of Lochcarron village is a small division of Lochcarron Products (of Galashiels) where you can see tartan still being handwoven. This process is really interesting and the sound of the loom is mesmerizing. After fingering the tartan in shops along the way, you will understand why the tartan produced here is extraordinary. This is heavy weight stuff. This is special order stuff, the stuff worn by the military and pipe bands. When you feel the weight, think what a proper man's 6 to 8 yard kilt would weigh.

Back on the road to Achnasheen, you'll feel like you are all alone in the hills as the road has dwindled down to one lane with turnouts. If you meet an on-coming car, then size up who is closer to a turnout, back up if you must, and be sure to give a wave to the other driver. This is really out there! Watch out for the sheep as they often lay on the warm pavement for their naps. A toot of the horn and a slow move forward will usually roust them, or you can jump out and wave your arms wildly and yell at them. The second method may or may not work. I've been given the evil eye by many a nasty looking and foul smelling sheep who could have cared less about my antics.

When you reach Achnasheen, you'll feel like you are back in civilization again and the trip down into Inverness is a snap.

I like taking this route for the sheer wildness of it. If you can go no farther north than Inverness, this side trip will give you the exhilaration of being alone on the land as many Scots still are today.

Western Highland Diversions – Hours & Directions

Loch Lomond is just off the A82 northwest of Glasgow. The highway follows the western bank of the loch. Balloch is on the A811 just a smidge from the A82.

Sweeney's Cruisers, Sweeney's Shipyard, 26 Balloch Rd, Balloch, Ph. 138.975.2376. Hour long cruises in summer start at 10:30am and the last sailing is 7:30pm. Cruises by demand in other seasons. Fee $$.

Inverarary Castle, Inveraray, Argyll. On the A83 about 1/2 mile from the village. Open April thru June, Sept. and Oct. Mon–Thurs and Sat 10am–1pm and 2pm-5:45pm, Sun. 1pm-5:45pm. During July and Aug. Mon–Sat 10am–5:45pm and Sun. 1pm–5:45pm. Fee $$. There is a giftshop, tearoom, and a nice picnic area.

Inverarary Jail, Church Square, Inveraray, Argyll. Open daily April thru Oct 9:30am-5pm and Nov thru Mar, 10am–4pm. Free.

Oban Distillery, Stafford Street, Oban, Argyll, Ph. 163.157.2004. Right downtown and only steps from the train station and the docks. Open year round Mon-Fri. 9:30am–5pm except Jul–Sept the closing time is 8:30pm. Easter to Oct. Saturday opening 9:30am–5pm. Dec thru Feb opening times may vary so call to confirm. Fee $.

Caithness Glass Company Factory Shop is located at the Railway Pier.

McCaig's Tower, on the hill overlooking Oban. You can't miss it! Free and open at all times. There is an observation tower on the seaward side. Fabuloso sunsets!!!

Oban Seal and Marine Centre, Barcaldine, Connel, Oban, Argyll. 10 miles north of Oban on the A828. Open year round, 10am–6pm except in July and Aug when hours are 9am–7pm. Fee $$$. Gift shop, restaurant, coffee shop, and picnic facilities.

Oban Rare Breeds Farm Park, New Barran, Oban, Argyll. 2 miles from Oban on the Glencruitten Road. Open late Mar thru Oct, 10am–5:30pm. Fee $$. Tearoom, picnic area, and gift shop. Woodland trail with great views.

Mull, Lynn of Lorne, Coll, and Tiree Ferry Service (and 19 other Islands), Caledonian MacBrayne ferries, Ph. 168.746. 2403. Not all of the 23 islands are served on a daily basis and weather can be a factor, so do your homework. If you are planning to stay on an island have reservations before you depart Oban.

Visitor Centre at Glencoe, Glencoe, Ballachulish, Argyll. On the A82, 17 miles south of Ft. William. The site is open all year round for free but the Visitor Centre is closed during the winter months. Open Mar-April and Sept-Oct daily 10am-5pm. May-Aug open daily 9:30am-5:30pm. Fee for Visitors Centre $$. Video program on the massacre and a mountaineering exhibit, snack bar and picnic area.

Glencoe Ski Centre, Kingshouse, Glencoe, Argyll. On the A82 30 miles south of Fort William. Open for skiing, Christmas to April. The chairlift and restaurant are open May–Sept for stunning views and back-country hikers. Fee $$.

West Highland Museum, Cameron Square, Ft. William. In the main downtown shopping district. Open, June-Sept, Mon-Sat 10am-5pm; July-Aug, Sun 2pm–5pm; Oct-May, Mon-Sat 10am-4pm. Fee $.

Ben Nevis and Ben Nevis Woollen Mill, Belford Road, Ft. William. 1/2 mile outside of Ft. William at the Glen Nevis entrance. Open year round. April-Oct, daily 9am-5pm; Nov-Mar 10am-4pm.

Ben Nevis Race, for details Ph. 139.770.4189.

Eilean Donan Castle, Dornie, Kyle of Lochalsh. 8 miles east of Kyle of Lochalsh on the A87. Open daily April thru Nov 10am–5:30pm. Fee $$. Very small, very cute. Gift shop and small tearoom.

Skye Museum of Island Life, Kilmuir, Isle of Skye. On the A855 five miles north of Uig. Open April thru Oct, Mon-Sat 9:30am-5:30pm. Fee $.

Haggisland is just off Wentworth Street. Hours as skittish as the wild haggis.

Dunvegan Castle, Dunvegan, Isle of Skye. On the A850, one mile north of the village of Dunvegan. Open daily Mar thru Oct, summer hours 10am-5:30pm, other times 11am-4pm. Fee $$$. Gift shop, restaurant, tearoom and picnic area. Boat trips are available to the seal colony.

Clan Donald Centre, located in the refurbished gardener's house on the grounds of Armadale Castle.

Armadale Castle Gardens and Museum of the Isles, Armadale Castle, Sleat, Isle of Skye. 21 miles south of the Skye Bridge on the A851 or 1 mile north of the

Armadale ferry terminal. Open daily April-Oct, 9:30am-5:30pm. Fee $$.

The 40 acre garden warmed by the gulf stream is within the Armadale Estate. World renowned amongst gardeners. If you are with a small group, the head gardener can be scheduled to give tours. Restaurant, Tearoom and gift shop. Another treat here are the Heavy Horse Tours. Horsedrawn dray takes you around the Armadale Estate and Gardens. Fee $$.

Skye Serpentarium, The Old Mill, Harrapool, Broadford, Isle of Skye. On the A850, 8 miles northwest of Kyleakin. Open Easter thru Oct, Mon–Sat 10am-5pm. During July and Aug and bank holidays, they are open on Sundays. Fee $. Gift shop and baby snakes for sale. Yahoo!

Lochcarron Products, Lochcarron. Take the road to Slumbay and Strome from the village. Weavers keep business hours during the week and longer hours during the summer. Free. Check out the view the weavers have! Incredible!!

~7~

The North, or more accurately The Northern Highlands

The Golf Courses:

West Coast: Ft. William, Lochcarron and Malliag
East Coast: Royal Dornoch, Brora, Golspie, Tain and Carnegie

Northern Highland Golf Courses

West Coast golf courses are few and far between with most of the courses around Ft. William. Your best bets are Ft. William, Lochcarron and Malliag.

The East Coast offers the most varied selection of courses and the best are centered around the Dornoch Firth. The much loved and treasured Royal Dornoch is the course to play in the far North, but a sample of the other excellent courses around the Firth are: Brora,

Golspie, Tain and the Carnegie Course at The Carnegie Club at Skibo Castle.

The importance of these courses to the East Coast is only too evident by looking at a current road map. Two new bridges have straightened and shortened the journey up the new motorway that ends right outside of the village of Dornoch. In 1905 King Edward VII made the trek to wee Dornoch and was so impressed that he gave the course the title Royal Dornoch. Even today the trek is long, and that is one reason why the British Open is not played here even though the course is outstanding.

The Northern Highlands

The Northern Highlands are a land unto themselves. From Inverness on the East Coast to Fort William on the West, the land is divided by a narrow valley in which Loch Ness, Loch Lochy and Loch Linneh lay connected by the Caledonian Canal. "Nessie", the Loch Ness Monster, could actually swim the width of the country from the North Sea to the Atlantic and be gone before a sharp-eyed scientist got the camera out. The vast country above this watery line is stunningly beautiful and desolate.

The remoteness of this part of the country is the reason you are here. If you need the constant stimulation of the city with all of the action only a city can provide, this may not be for you. But if you will happily wait for a sheep to decide to get up and out of the road, or want to wait for that perfect sunset over a loch, or get a kick out of watching fishermen getting the catch ashore, this is just your ticket.

Remember, once you leave Inverness you are in a part of the country that is extremely remote and the population is very small, not many more than 30,000 souls, so don't expect a wide variety of choices in lodging, meals, or evening entertainment.

Inverness –

Capital of The Highlands

It seems all roads north eventually funnel into the largest city in the north of Scotland, Inverness. The city itself isn't that interesting, but it is a wonderful stopping place for recharging from a hectic whirl of historic buildings and scenic grandeur.

If you have driven the road along Loch Ness and missed sighting the elusive Loch Ness Monster, then you may want to take one of the many water tours offered on Loch Ness. They are quite economical and could really pay off if you get a clear snapshot or video of Nessie. Jacobite Cruises doesn't guarantee sightings but their combined boat/coach tour will probably take you to visit The Official Monster Exhibition and the competing Original Visitor Centre in Drumnadrochit.

Inverness Castle sits above the River Ness in the heart of town but, unlike the majestic castles in Sterling and Edinburgh, this "castle" is a small, municipal building built of pinkish sandstone in the mid 1800s. Flora MacDonald, who helped Bonnie Prince Charlie escape the English army after the Battle of Culloden in 1746, is memorialized by a statue in front of the castle. She appears to be shading her eyes and squinting. Could she be trying to comprehend her predicament of being forever frozen in front of a pink police station? The castle shares a hilltop location with the Inverness Museum and Art Gallery which has a nice collection of artifacts depicting Highland Life, including an impressive collection of Highland silver. The castle's lawns, stretching down to the riverbank, are a wonderful place to have your take-away lunch before marching down into the town for a good look-around.

For any enthusiast of the bagpipe or other Scottish ethnic music, be sure not to miss Balnain House of Highland Music. Housed in an elegant Georgian mansion built in 1726, this house was pressed into service as a hospital after the Battle of Culloden but now music has brought it happier times. There are audio and visual displays to keep one's toes tapping for hours, and a shop stocked with instruments, sheet music, cassettes, CDs and a knowledgeable staff. An extensive list of classes is offered in everything from stepdancing, penny whistle and the intricacies of pibrocht. During the summer months, musical events are scheduled on most evenings.

The last great battle fought on British soil was the Battle of Culloden (April 16, 1746) fought between the Jacobites, led by Bonnie Prince Charlie Stuart, and the Hanoverian Army led by the Duke of Cumberland (aka "Butcher of Cumberland"). It only took forty minutes of battle to forever change the history and rule of Scotland.

The National Trust for Scotland maintains the battlefield and a superb informational center. You can walk out onto the moor to view the front lines and the mass graves with their clan markers. This really will give you pause.

Shopping is excellent in Inverness, from a huge mall just southeast of the city that may make you believe you haven't left home to my favorite place to prowl, the old Victorian Market, a twisty clutter of buildings connected by covered walkways. You'll find everything from fresh rabbit for stew to one-of-a-kind hand spun and knit sweaters. I like looking down dark corridors and up little stairways so as not to miss tiny shops that have antique prints and used books. I've found miniscule stores in the morning that I could not find again in the afternoon. It is like being on a treasure hunt but you can also easily find a pizza or good coffee to fortify yourself without leaving the market.

If you are in need of Highland dress, Inverness may be the place to look. There are several major firms specializing in just that. A local family owned shop, Duncan Chisholm and Sons, can have you completely outfitted from in-stock inventory or you can be measured for custom sizes and obscure tartans. D&H Norval, the best jewelry store in town, has high quality and unusual Highland and Celtic styles for something other than what you see in most of the tourist venues.

James Pringle Weavers, just a short jaunt from town, welcomes you to their mill where they have been producing fine tweed, tartan and knitwear since 1798. They have a huge mill shop with many Scottish producers represented.

If you are looking for original artwork one of the best galleries featuring Scots themes is Riverside Gallery.

Inverness offers a huge range of evening entertainment. There are several "Scottish Night" type events available for the traditional touristy bagpipe/accordion/sword dance/sing-a-long fun. The brochure for Scottish Showtime promises "dance, music, and mirth" or you could try something quite different. How different? Well…

Roller Bowl, Bingo at The Carlton, or water sports and slides at Aquadome. For a bit more traditional fare the modern Eden Court Theatre features live theater, music and dance year-round.

Lodging In And Around Inverness

Brae Ness Hotel, (Ness Bank, Inverness IV2 4SF, Ph. 146.371.2266, Fax 146.323.1732) is directly across the river from Inverness Castle. You may want to ask for a castle view room. Median priced.

Glen Mhor Hotel and Restaurant, (9-12 Ness Bank, Inverness IV2 4SG, Ph. 146.323.4308, Fax 146.371.3170) is one block east of the castle with a view across the river to St. Andrew's Cathedral and the Eden Court Theatre. Median priced.

Talisker, (25 Ness Bank, Inverness IV2 4SF, Ph. 146.3 23.6221) is just down the block from the Glen Mohr. This family run Victorian house is a convenient and economical bed and breakfast within easy walking distance of the town center.

Aros, (Mrs. Ann Petrie, Aros, 5 Abertarff Rd., Inverness IV2 2NW, Ph. 146.323.5674) a 5 minute walk to town and railway station this charming Victorian bed and breakfast, located in a very nice neighborhood, is a balm to your budget.

Culloden House Hotel, (Milton of Culloden, Inverness IV2 7BZ, Toll free from the US 1.800.373.7987, Fax 146.3 79.2181) has my vote for the splurge. A gorgeous Georgian mansion laden with Virginia creeper is near the Culloden Battlefield. If this place is good enough for Bonnie Prince Charlie, Charles Windsor and the Crown Prince of Japan, it will suffice for me. Notice I said "will". I'll need a bank account transfusion first.

Inverness Diversions –

Hours & Directions

Jacobite Cruises, Tomnahurich Bridge, Glenurquhart Road, Inverness IV3 5TD, Ph. 146.323.3999. Calednonia Canal and Loch Ness cruise and coach tours. Open year round. Fee $$.

The Official Monster Exhibition, The Drumnadrochit Hotel, Drumnadrochit, Ph. 145.645.0573. History and current exploration for Nessie are both documented. Boat trips out onto the lake arranged. Fee $$$. NOTE: I haven't recommended this hotel because the last time I visited the smell of smoke and stale beer almost knocked me over. Maybe they've had a good spring clean since.

The Original Visitor Centre, Loch Ness Lodge Hotel, Drumnadrochit, Ph. 145.645.0342. The display here centers around a cinema show in a 180 person theater. Fee $$.

Inverness Castle, Castle Wynd. Court house and administrative offices. Open during business hours.

Inverness Museum and Art Gallery, Castle Wynd, Inverness. Across the street from Inverness Castle. Open all year except public holidays, Mon-Sat 9am-5pm. Free.

Balnain House of Highland Music, 40 Huntly Street, Inverness. Located on the banks of the River Ness the house can be reached by a 5 minute walk from the town center. Open year round. July-Aug, Mon-Fri 10am–10pm, Sat-Sun 10am-6pm; Sept-June, Mon-Sat 10am-5pm. Fee $. Special events and Ceilidhs throughout the summer.

Culloden Battlefield, Visitor Center, Culloden Moor, Inverness. Located 5 miles east of Inverness on the B9006. Feb-Mar and Nov-Dec 10am-4pm; Apr-Oct 9am-6pm; closed in January. Fee $$.
The battlefield is open at all times. Free.

Victorian Martket, Oh God! This is an area without a definite address. It wanders around behind the shops on the north side of Bridge and High Streets. Ask for directions.

Duncan Chisholm and Sons, 47-53 Castle Street, Inverness. If you've never seen fabric kilted, ask to see their workroom if a kilt is being worked on. This is really an amazing process.

D&H Norval Jewellers, 88 Church Street, Inverness.

James Pringle Weavers, Holm Mills, Dores Road, Inverness. On the B862 just 1.5 miles southwest of Inverness. Open daily Mar-Oct, 9am-5:30pm; Nov-Dec, 9am-5pm; and Jan-Feb 10am-5pm. Free.

Riverside Gallery, 11 Bank Street, Inverness.

Scottish Showtime, The Cummings Hotel, Church Street, Inverness. Showtime Hotline 134.983.0930. Early June to late Sept, Mon-Sat 8:30pm.

Roller Bowl, 167 Culduthel Road, Inverness. What's better than snacks and bowling? Open year round, Mon-Fri Noon 'til late and Sat-Sun 11am 'til late.

Bingo at The Carlton, 18 Huntly Street, Inverness. Game sessions happen throughout the day and into the evenings. There is a full service bar and bistro so you can play to your heart's content.

Aquadome, Bught Park, Inverness. The competition pool opens at 7:30am for lap swim and is open into the evening. School groups may have priority at times. The "leisure waters" - slides, wave pool and lazy river - are open from 10am-9pm on weekdays and 9am-8pm on weekends. There is a health center, café, and beauty salon on premise. Fees $ - $$$.

Eden Court Theatre, Bishop's Road, Inverness, Fax 146.3 71.3810. Varied programs throughout the year. Art gallery also on premise.

Dornoch

This tiny village is picture postcard perfect - a Scotland in miniature. Tidy cottages and little gardens literally wrap around its' heart - the 13th Century Dornoch Cathedral. Dornoch Castle, now a hotel, is just across the street from the Cathedral, and down the street is the town jail, now <u>The Dornoch Craft Center</u> operated by one of Scotland's premier woolen manufacturers. There are cute little antique shops that cater to golf widows, a small Spar grocery store and tiny shops that have nothing to do with the golf - only village life. Check out the windows of the shops and pubs for upcoming entertainments or needs. One sign announced "Extra Yarn needed for Animal Shelter Beds Project". Now there was a conversation just waiting to happen.

The <u>Royal Dornoch Golf Course</u>, the "St. Andrews of the North," is within easy walking distance of the village center. It just seems to flow out of its neighbor's back gardens and the farmer's fields. No fanfare here, just golf overlooked by a musty looking hotel and hemmed in on the east by a gorgeous, long sandy beach.

Lodging In Dornoch

As you might tell I love this village. I do! My first night was at the castle, and at a friend's recommendation my second night was in an old, family run Victorian Hotel, and I was hooked.

<u>Dornoch Castle Hotel</u> (Castle St., Dornoch, IV25 3SD, Ph. 186.281.0216, Fax 186.281.0981) has extremely reasonable rates for a castle, and a wee bar worth toasting. The bar is dark, tiny, medieval and warmed by a huge fireplace ... a terrific place to settle for a meal and an evening's conversation that the whole bar takes part in because of the size. The afternoon and evening I spent in

the bar was so entertaining. There was a wedding going on somewhere in the village. Several young couples were staying in the hotel and they seemed to have arranged a pre-reception event in the bar. These young people were dressed beautifully – the men in full dress kilts and the women in lovely gowns. This was a truly romantic sight in the castle setting.

I also met a young man who had traveled to the far Outer Hebrides and was nursing a broken heart about having to leave for his home in New Jersey the next day. He had a wealth of information about an isolated part of the world where I have never ventured.

Dornoch Castle has 6 rooms within the original castle and 11 rooms in a new wing. The new wing looks out over the garden, which is charming, but the old rooms are much more fun.

Burghfield House Hotel (Dornoch, Sutherland, Ph. 186.281.0212, Fax 186.281.0404) is indeed my idea of heaven. This hotel is situated in lovely gardens and has been seen to for generations by a loving family. The reception hall is all dark wood and balustered stairwell. The Guest's Lounge is large and with decor so exquisite *House Beautiful* could walk in and do a photo shoot with no warning. Scarlet O'Hara and Maria von Trapp made dresses from curtains, but these draperies would get you on Mr. Blackwell's Best Dressed List. And when I thought I'd died and gone to heaven, the owner swept into the lounge and began introducing me, by name, to the other guests. That evening, and far into the night, my new friends, their dogs and I sat in the clubby Lounge Bar and watched The Master's live from Atlanta, Georgia.

Did I mention waking to snow on Easter morning? Nothing could have been more romantic ... well ... Sean Connery would have been a plus, but never mind.

American industrialist Andrew Carnegie retired to Skibo Castle (Dornoch, IV25 3RQ, Ph. 186.289.4600, Fax 186.289.4601) a Scottish Baronial Style Extravaganza, to enjoy his millions and his Scottish Heritage. The castle is now operated as an exclusive sporting club for a wealthy, international clientel who are invited to join. Madonna's wedding party and her guests stayed here, and I hate to imagine the bill with rooms starting at $935 for members. Rooms are available on a one time only nonmember price, in the range of $1,500 per night including meals, drinks and golf. It is worth a peek and a drink. I'd recommend not wearing your jeans unless you actually are Madonna. If you can afford to join (approximately $5,100 per year per family) and decide to spend a week, give me a call. I'll carry your bags.

Dornoch Diversions –

Hours & Directions

Dornoch Cathedral, Castle Square. Open daily 9am til dusk. Daily services are held here so please be polite and quiet.

Dornock Craft Centre, Town Jail, Castle Street, Dornoch IV25 3SD. Craft Shop open year-round 9:30am–5pm Monday thru Friday. Saturdays from Easter thru September, and Sundays in July and August 12pm–5pm. There is a café featuring home baking in the former Governor's Room.

The Road to John O'Groats

If you are going to the northerly tip of Scotland, there is basically one road with a loop at its end. I told you there weren't many choices.

I've never gone farther than Thurso on the Coast road and I've never cut across country to the northwest coast either. One day I will and I'll bet that my presence could possibly double the population in some wee spots.

Along the coast road there are very few major roadside attractions. The wild Highland and cliffed North Sea vistas will more than suffice. Your company in the car will be Norwegian and Scots Gaelic radio and you'll know you're not in Kansas anymore, Dorothy.

Dunrobin Castle

Just northeast of the cheery little town of Golspie is the ancestral home of the earls and dukes of Sutherland. The vista from their terrace at <u>Dunrobin Castle</u> is a dandy way to start your trip north or an easy day trip out of Dornoch. This turreted, storybook castle overlooking the sea is still lived in and cared for by the original family. The Dukes and Duchesses must have known that if they were to entice houseguests this far north, they had to have something for them to do and this house actually feels like a good time was had by all. The grand stair from the dark and freezing cold entrance hall is filled with antlers with the hunter's name engraved on individual brass plaques, and at the top of the stair is a huge billiards room. You can just imagine the smokey, boozey conversations and laughter this house has heard.

Besides the house, there are formal, French gardens, wooded walks, a new bird of prey center and just down the lane, a little pavilion where the spoils of many a Duke's travels are stored. Tusks, pelts, models of boats, native costumes and weapons are piled in this little building. I wonder if the Duchesses made the Dukes keep their stuff out there?

Grey Cairns of Camster

Unless you are starving for one of the best steak dinners on this earth, don't take the A9 to Wick and Thurso because you'll miss the puny little one lane road to the <u>Grey Cairns of Camster</u>. Watch for the sign at West Clyth and don't panic, this road does actually go to a Neolithic (4000-1800 BC) pile of rocks that was an apartment complex. While you are driving over these boggy hills, think about the ancient wheat fields that graced this once near desert land. A raised boardwalk will keep you out of the wet, marshy muck as you move toward two chambered cairns that look like rounded piles of stones. These piles were once communal dwellings for the farmers of the region. As you get closer, you will see there are no windows only small doors. It's a shame the residents couldn't look out on the waving fields of wheat from this high point but I suppose enjoyment of views wasn't something you could indulge in 5000 years ago. This is truly an awe-inspiring experience.

Continue on this little road, taking time to wait out the aloof sheep, and you'll pass isolated, sparkling white farmhouses sitting on a broad plain. Soon you'll see road signs again pointing you to Thurso and the best darned steak dinner this side of Harry Carey's in Chicago.

Thurso

Thurso is the most northerly point served by British Rail, and this far north, you've pretty much left the tartan and touristy kitsch behind. You'll find Thurso is like a town in the outback of Montana. It's a rough and tumble kind of town that clings to the landscape with great determination. It isn't pretty or quaint, but it is real and the folks are fond of Americans and sad for having lost their "American Base" (U.S. Navy) several years ago.

Now for that steak dinner I've been talking about. The Ferry Inn of Scrabster (a short drive or cab ride) is so good you should make reservations as soon as you hit Thurso and try to get a window seat. The restaurant is pressed up against the base of a sheer cliff and shares precious real estate with the Orkney and Shetland ferries and fishing fleet. Head for the Upper Deck for a view of the port and tuck into a solid meal. I'm sure the seafood is fresh off the boat but the steaks are Scottish beef and cooked to an American's taste. And for dessert, I'm sure we have some Yankee sailor's wife to thank for the Kentucky Grasshopper Pie.

John O'Groats vs

Dunnet Head

Most travelers come this far north to say they've been to the farthest northerly tip of mainland Britain - John O'Groats. They'd be wrong by a few very breathtaking miles. Dunnet Head is a very desolate headland with deadly cliffs plunging straight down. If the weather is not co-operating, you can sit right at the edge of the cliff in your car and see the Orkneys in the distance. For some reason I thought of just about every film I'd ever seen where cars go over the cliff, so I parked back a ways and walked to the view. This is the end, the very end of mainland Britain. There is a lighthouse here and that's it.

Now to satisfy your friends we're off to John O'Groats where you can have your picture taken in front of a signpost pointing toward home and displaying the mileage to get there (a very clever idea). The photographer's dog will wait patiently for you to have your photo snapped and then you can throw his soccer ball. It's an added benefit to a stop here.

You can have the "last cup of tea" at the "last café," buy the "last postcard" at the "last souvenir shop" and visit the "last house" here in John O'Groats, but don't miss a new collection of buildings that houses the working studios and sales rooms of local craftspeople.

If you decide to spend the night in John O' Groats it will be like spending the night on a desert island. Your choices for lodging and entertainment are extremely limited but your welcome will be warm wherever you choose to go. The Lythe Arts Centre, just outside of John O'Groats, is a converted country school that offers an ever-changing smorgasbord of arts and entertainment and a pleasant change from another pub crawl.

We've been as far as we can go north, so let's head down the road and see what we've missed on the way up.

Wick and Then South Again

Wick, the largest town north of Inverness, is the business heart of the Northern Highlands and the town is busy. Major shopping brings people from miles and miles around and the Safeway parking lot seems like a party.

Caithness Glass - You've admired it in all the finest shops and here you are, in its hometown. Prices are pretty standard around the country but I've found some fabulous buys on the sale table at this state of the art factory.

Wick Heritage Centre - Wick once was the center for a huge fishing fleet that went after herring. See what the extremely prosperous town was like before the fall of the fisheries.

<u>Northlands Viking Centre</u> (Auckengill) - You've been listening to Norwegian radio so you know it's close by. Those stouthearted Vikings rowed across the North Sea and left a lasting impression on this coast.

<u>Laidhay Croft Museum</u> - You've been seeing these long white houses throughout the country and here is your chance to get inside and see what the living was like. I was surprised. If the museum isn't open, call at the house at the end of the car park and the nice residents will pry themselves away from their spectacular view to open the museum for you. A donation is appreciated.

<u>Dunbeath Heritage Centre</u> - If you are doing your family's historical research in this part of Scotland, this is the place you want to visit. There are nice displays from Bronze to today's Oil Age.

<u>Hill O' Many Stanes</u>, near Lybster - and they ain't kiddin'. Lottsa stanes, laid out in a pattern on a sloping hillside by some Stone Age folks. Beats me, but it sure is interesting (viewing time 2 mins. or less).

Helmsdale

The tiny little town of Helmsdale has a nice restaurant where I was informed that there was no fish on the menu because the boat hadn't returned yet, but they were expecting to have fish on the evening menu. The apple tart with custard was tasty and I'll go back to the Bunillidh Restaurant and its cozy fireplace. To live in this part of the country you have to diversify your living, and the nice folks at the Bunillidh Restaurant also offer lodging, The <u>Timespan Museum</u>, an award winning heritage center, and <u>The Grotto</u>, in the basement, touts octopus and bibles as featured attractions. These enterprising folk will arrange for you to eat fish, to catch fish or to pan gold at <u>Baile an Or</u> where there was a gold rush in 1869.

North of Dornoch Diversions - Hours & Directions

<u>Dunrobin Castle</u>, one half mile northeast of Golspie, Ph.140.863.3177. Twelve miles north of Dornoch on the A9. Hours: April, May, and Oct 10:30am–4:30pm Mon–Sat and Sun noon til 4pm. June thru Sept 10:30am-5pm daily. Fee $$. The Bird of Prey exhibit is open the same hours.

<u>Grey Cairns of Camster</u>, 5 miles north of Lybster, turn at the Watten Road. Watch for the sign. 8 miles of single track road - don't give up. Site is open year round. No Fee. No facilities, just rocks and sheep.

<u>The Ferry Inn</u>, Scrabster. 2 miles north of Thurso.

<u>Lyth Arts Centre</u>, between Wick and John O'Groats off the A9, Ph. 195.564.1270. The Gallery opens daily during July and Aug, 2pm-4:30pm. Open year round for scheduled performances and activities.

Caithness Glass, Airport Industrial Estate, Wick, Ph 195.560.2286. Northwest outskirts of town. Hours: Open all year Mon–Sat 9am-5pm. Open Sundays Easter thru Dec 11am-5pm. Free. Good showroom shopping, restaurant and factory tours.

Wick Heritage Centre, 20 Bank Row, Wick, Ph. 195.560.5393. Open May thru Sept, Mon–Sat 10am-5pm. Fee $.

Northlands Viking Centre, Auckengill, Keiss, Wick, Ph. 195.560.7771. Open daily June thru Sept 10am-4pm. Fee $. Located 10 miles north of Wick on the A99. There is bus service to Auckengill.

Laidhay Croft Museum, Laidhay, Dunbeath, Caithness, Ph 159.373.1244. Open daily the last two weeks in Mar and then April thru Oct and the first 2 weeks in Nov. Hours are 10am-6pm. Fee $. Located on the A9 one mile north of Dunbeath. Picnic area and tearoom and spectacular North Sea views.

Dunbeath Heritage Centre, Old School. Dunbeath, Caithness, Ph 159.373.1233. Open daily 11am-5pm April-Sept. Fee $.

Hill O' Many Stones, Mid Clyth 4 miles northeast of Lybster. Watch for the sign on the A9 indicating the turnoff. Free for the gazing. No facilities just rocks.

Bunillidh Restaurant & Bed and Breakfast (2 – 4 Dunrobin Street, Helmsdale, Ph. 143.182.1457). Open year round for breakfast, lunch, dinner and even a good bed.

164

Fresh seafood, at times local game, and a vegetarian menu are available.

Time Span Museum, Dunrobin St., Helmsdale, Sutherland, Ph. 143.182.1327. Open April thru Oct, Mon-Sat 9:30am-5pm and Sun 2pm-5pm and often later in the summer months. Fee $$. Award winning audio-visual displays and a gallery featuring revolving exhibitions of contemporary artists.

The Grotto, In the basement of the Bunillidh Restaurant. Free. Funky and Fun displays.

Baile an Or, 4 miles northwest of Helmsdale on the A897. Rent gold panning equipment in Helmsdale. Who knows, you might strike it rich.

~8~

A Long Drive Right Up The Center
Edinburgh to Inverness

The Golf Courses:

Gleneagles, Crieff, Pitlochery and Kingussie

This alternate drive North involves not much more than choosing the right driver and going for it. Straight up the M90 from Edinburgh, across the Firth of Forth Bridge, and a slight dogleg at Perth onto the A9 will land you on Inverness Castle Green in about 3 hours. You'll have seen some stunning mountain scenery on the way north, but you'll also have missed so many delightful, little diversions along the way. My advice is to get off the freeway often and watch for signs painted on old tires saying "Caution Wee Lambs", gaze at lakes so mirror-like that the reflections give you vertigo, or stop and yell encouragement to kayakers navigating a thundering mountain stream.

I think the best way to make "the long drive" is by aiming at points of interest along the route. Some of these diversions are out of the question if you don't have a car or time enough to take a rural bus, but I will tell you when they are reachable by train.

Once again, if you have a golfer riding shot gun, while polishing his wedge, you will be pleased by the choices available to be rid of him along the way. The golf courses here are not the windswept links of the seaside but rolling parkland or hilly mountainside courses.

Now, I think I'll take you on several of the little diversions I've found on my way to The North.

You may be wondering about my use of the term "The North". All along the main motorways and highways of Scotland you will see the term being used. It is helpful, if on your way north, you see a sign pointing to "The North" in your rearview mirror. You'll know you've botched something up at the last roundabout. Don't ask me how I know this.

Stirling

Stirling is a perfect change of pace from the big urban centers of Edinburgh and Glasgow and approximately 40 miles from both. This small city / large town is easily accessible by bus and train with many arrivals and departures each day.

Once the seat of government of Scotland, Stirling has a castle perched high above a lush green plane where Sir William Wallace and King Robert The Bruce fought the English, and eventually won independence at the Battle of Stirling Bridge in 1297 and Bannockburn in 1314. There are monuments large and small around the town to commemorate these grand moments in Scottish history. The Bannockburn Heritage Centre is right on the battlefield and since Mel Gibson painted his face blue and donned a kilt to play Wallace in *Braveheart,* the attendance at this site has been tremendous.

When you visit Stirling Castle leave your car in a lot at the bottom of the hill and take the Back Walk, a steady uphill walking path. For a closer look at the Old Town, I recommend starting up King Street, a one way up street, that eventually becomes Spittal, St. John, and then Castlehill Wynd. You can park right up at the castle but you'll be dodging tour buses and crowds, and more importantly you'd miss poking into the medieval alleys, lanes, and wynds you'll pass on the way up. Sixteenth and seventeenth century houses and civic buildings, refurbished and serving well in the 21st Century, are the norm in this Old Town center. The Castle Ticket Booth/Tourist Office/Gift Shop has a little secret that is fun to find. There, in the back of the shop, is a window that cantilevers out and you get a fabulous view of the cliff drop off, the plane below and hey, isn't that a golf course down there?

Another plus at the ticket booth is combined admission to the Castle and Argyll's Lodging, so don't throw out your ticket.

As a working military garrison Stirling Castle had been long neglected but now it is a work in progress with construction everywhere. Areas that have been completed have been called "Disneyesque," but I found it a delightful change of pace from just gazing at furnished rooms.

The kitchens have been finished and you'll feel like you've walked in on dinner preparations. There are baskets of fowl and fish, looking so real you expect them to move. Very lifelike men are carrying a deer to the spit, the chef is chopping, maids are squabbling, and you hear the sound as you approach each area. The lighting is as dim as it would have been in the period and the whole effect is very, very interesting.

Other areas of the castle are under construction or awaiting finishing touches, so the castle feels very alive. The only downer for me was the <u>Regimental Museum of the Argyll and Sutherland Highlanders</u>. A proud military regiment, putting on a "bully for us" face to war, was just tired and too sad. I'll get down off the soapbox now because you may be a Boer War expert and this could be just the bees knees.

Turn right as you leave the castle gates and walk down Castlehill Wynd, stopping first at <u>Valley Cemetery</u>. You won't be waking the dead, for I'm sure their ghosts are enjoying the view from Lady Rock that looks directly at the castle. Hold onto your socks and have film in the camera.

Leaving the cemetery, you need only cross the street to <u>Argyll's Lodging</u>. The Duke of Argyll, needing a home near the castle, remodelled this old town house in 1670, and even the crew of *This Old House* would be impressed with the restoration. Today, not all of the rooms are furnished but there is a wonderful audio/visual presentation, winding stairs, and charming views from the windows.

The gift shop contains carefully chosen arts and crafts that reflect the period of the house. Pewter, tapestry, embroidery and jewelry abound, but tartan Nessies were few and far between in this little room.

When you leave the house, turn down the hill again and visit <u>The Church of The Holy Rude</u> where Mary Queen of Scots' 13 month old son was crowned James VI in 1567. Services are still held in the church that has been artfully preserved.

Lodging In Stirling

Once again, a visit to the Tourist Office at the Castle gates presented a bright little B&B run by the MacDonalds, an elderly couple who took an active interest in their guests. I liked that they made introductions at breakfast so I didn't sit like a stone next to the German couple at the next table.

When you leave Sterling resume the journey north on the A9 you will come to...

Auchterarder

A funny name for a cute, little farm town but who supports the fancy clothing stores, gift shops, and antique shops? Golf Widows!

Gleneagles Golf Course and Hotel sits in all of its stuffy glamour just outside of the town. Like Turnberry, in the southwest, this is "the" golf course of the region but unlike Turnberry, golf isn't the only reason for its existence. There are 4 championship golf courses and a golf academy on the property, but "sport" is king here and you may not even touch a club with all the options.

Mark Phillips, Princess Anne's ex-husband, runs the riding stables. You may like to try clay pigeon shooting at the Jackie Stewart (of Formula One racing fame) School of Shooting and Fishing. Or how about the 4x4 Off Road Course so you can improve your minivan skills?

The Gleneagles Hotel (Auchterarder PH3 1NF, Ph. 176.466.2231, Fax 176.469.4387 and e-mail resort.sales@gleneagles.com) is extremely plush in a "smart set", stuck-up sort of way. The building itself was built in the 1920s and looks more like a large hospital or sanitarium in a novel of that period. Don't get me wrong, it is lovely but it just feels very dark, contrived and businesslike to me. However, Gleneagles will not miss me, as there are scads of people who can afford the starting room rate of $500 or a $150 round on the golf course.

Auchterarder town does offer a full range of hotels, guest houses and B&Bs to ease the pain.

Crieff

Getting real about life after Gleneagles, you may as well happily try the Victorian resort town of Crieff. You'll need a car or the local bus as there is no train service to Crieff.

This area offers up at least one of everything you need for a perfect vacation plus 6 golf courses. The castle and gardens – Drummond – are just down the road while Glenturret Distillery, the oldest in Scotland, is on the road to Lock Earn where you can enjoy sparkling vistas and water sports. There is the Wildlife and Highland Cattle Centre, ancient monuments and numerous walking and hiking trails in the hills.

And then there is my favorite stop: The Crieff Visitor Center encompasses what every Golf Widow loves – factory stores!!! Buchan Thistle Pottery and Perthshire Paperweights have their factories right here along with a crowded restaurant and popular garden center. Across the street, Stuart Crystal is my all time great bargain hunting spot. You can watch glass being blown and cut in the factory and then shop till you drop in the showroom. I came home with crystal wine bottle stoppers which turned out to be show stoppers and not more than 6 bucks each!

Back in the town center is one of the finest retail art galleries in all of Scotland. The Strathern Gallery features original paintings, jewelry and sculpture by local and nationally known artists. If high quality artwork is on your "souvenir" list, then I can highly recommend this gallery.

Lodging In Crieff

Lots of Victorians did their holiday making in Crieff, but long before that, in 1745, Bonnie Prince Charlie stayed at the Drummond Arms (James Square, Crieff PH7 3HX, Ph. 176.465.2151) and plotted strategy with his generals for the ill fated Battle of Culloden. The Drummond Arms, right on the main square, isn't fancy but old fashioned and the funky ambiance works for me. I swear the Bonnie Prince was just one week too early to ride in the lift (just kidding) that clanks and shudders along its 3 floor route as if it were 250 years old.

The food at the Drummond Arms is plain but very tasty, and I say that you should try the Banoffey Pudding. If there is a sing-a-long in the bar, join in and become part of the regulars.

Just up the hill near the ultra-posh Crieff Hydro Hotel and Golf Course (Crieff PH7 3LQ, Ph. 176.465.5555) is the Murraypark Hotel (Connaught Terrace, Crieff PH7

3DJ, Ph. 176.465.5311. This large, pink stone home has had some remodeling that gives it a really friendly, casual clubhouse feel. The rooms are attractive, the dining room is extra good with nice views into the garden, and there is a sitting room/lounge for after dinner coffee and conversation. The little bar is usually alive with golfers bragging about their day's score so take your drink out to the lounge.

When you are ready to leave Crieff you can make two very different direction decisions.

To the east on the A85 you will be able to drive directly west into Oban on the Atlantic coast. This road will take you past Loch Earn, a pristine mountain lake, through Lochearnhead, a small mountain resort, and then on into a very rugged, unpopulated stretch of highway before reaching Kilchurn Castle. The road is good and the goal of Oban is worthwhile. This route is especially good if you can't go farther north. You will find great little towns and villages and rugged Highland scenery without a long drive, and you'll be able to take the coast road back south to Glasgow.

Leaving Crieff on the A822, you'll be heading north again through forestland. You'll make very good time on this road because there are very few houses, let alone a town and you can regain the A9 highway at Dunkeld for a quick trip into Pitlochry.

Pitlochry and Killiecrankie

Back on the A9 you will be steadily climbing into the Highlands, and the forested hills will start to close in around the highway and the train line. Pitlochry has long been a destination for outdoor enthusiasts and there are excellent hiking trails available. If you aren't into heady outdoor adventure, you will be well pleased that the Pitlochry Festival Theatre has a full schedule from May through October. You can see live theatre and music, sometimes twice a day, during the summer.

Pitlochry is unusual in that it is almost entirely gray stone, not more than two stories high and appears to be one long street. This one long street is jammed with clothing shops, ice cream vendors, novelty stores, and at the far north end wall-to-wall hotels and B&Bs for the steady stream of holiday makers.

Dining In Pitlochry

I spent one dreamy night at Il Pontevecchio (Ferry Road, Pitlochry, Ph 179.647.4400), just off the main road near the train station. The place was filled with lovers and I was plunked down right by the kitchen. This sounds like a single woman's most common bad dream, doesn't it? It was not. The owner and the waiter, both Italian, and the Italian trained Scots chef made me feel so special that I could have been sitting out by the dumpster and had a grand time. The next morning I saw the waiter on the street and we exchanged hugs and air kisses like old friends. I know I drank way too much wine, but I will never forget the meal and these charming men who dropped off little plates full of sample bites of the entrees which were headed to the other diners.

Lodging In Pitlochry

Tons of great little places of character are available here. I stayed in the <u>Carra Beag Guest House</u> (16 Toberargan Road, Pitlocry PH16 5HG, Ph. 179.647.2835) run by a young family. Helen Fox and Brian Stone seemed to be enjoying their house full of foreign guests while they ran at full speed. Not fancy but very convenient and fun.

If you're looking for a little less casual then try the small <u>Port-na-Craig Inn</u> (Pitlochry PH16 5EG, Ph. 179.647.2777), right on Loch Tummel and adjacent to the Festival Theatre.

Also on the road to Loch Tummel, you'll find an old coaching inn, Loch Tummel Inn (Strathtummel, By Pitlochry PH16 5RP, Ph. 188.263.4272) and Bonskeid House Holiday and Conference Center (By Pitlochry PH16 5NP, Ph. 179.647.3208). The Bonskeid is an old baronial home with all the turrets and towers you'd expect of a baron. The price is extremely reasonable, reflecting the fact that not all the rooms have en-suite bathrooms but they do have a tennis court.

Killiecrankie

God I love the sound of that word! The Pass of Killiecrankie is just north of Pitlochry and the best pub around is in the Killiecrankie Hotel (Pass of Killiecrankie, By Pitlocry PH16 5LG, Ph.179.647.3220.) which also offers up some very nice rooms. Don't look for much else in Killiecrankie besides good mountain air.

Blair Atholl

The tiny village of Blair Atholl has Blair Castle to thank for its main existence. There are some nice, small hotels and residences serving up B&B to the visitors who come to see the striking home of the Dukes of Atholl. The current Duke resides here with his family and the estate is a hard working farm besides being Scotland's most visited, privately owned home.

The Dukes of Atholl have always had a private army, the last remaining in Britain, and you'll see evidence of the army throughout the house in the form of suits of armor, swords, axes, and unwieldy muskets mounted in interesting designs on the walls. Hopefully the current regiment has been updated.

Also mounted on the walls are antlers and more antlers and one particular hallway has antlers mounted on bubblegum pink walls above a red carpet. I guess you'll have to see it for yourself before you can decide if the combo works.

The gardens surrounding Blair Castle are a work in progress. There is a brand new walled water garden with incredible sculpture, and when you walk out on the well-marked forest paths, you'll find trees that have fallen or purposely felled only to have their stumps transformed into mushrooms or animal carvings. This is a terrific place to picnic.

Now get back onto the A9 and enjoy the mountain scenery on your way to Inverness. No… there are a couple of stops that may catch your fancy, so I'd better tell you about them.

Kingussie and Newtonmore

If you are a MacPherson you may want to make a wee stop in these two villages which are just off the A9. There is a <u>Clan MacPherson House Museum</u> and two Highland folklife museums. Newtonmore's <u>Folklife Museum</u> is open air to support the reconstructed or restored Highland farm buildings that you can wander freely. Kingussie's <u>Highland Folklife Museum</u> is open air to support the reconstructed… Hey wait a minute! These two are completely separate facilities within a stones throw of one another. Do you think there is a family feud or town rivalry going on?

Kingussie also has a golf course if you need one for yourself or your car companion.

Aviemore

What appears to be a warren of newish hotels sharing parking lots is actually one of Scotland's premier resort destinations. Aviemore, with the help of the snow gods, is a winter ski resort, but it is also a year round convention center with all the amenities to keep the family happy. Indoor swimming pools, an ice rink, amusement arcades, and nonstop evening entertainment supplement the great outdoor facilities. For many weeks out of the year, the place is booked tighter than a tick and it really isn't the place I'd choose to stay, but there are two great attractions that could tempt you to stop.

The Cairngorm Chair Lift takes you, in two stages, to 3600 feet and the summit of Cairngorm Peak. The view is spectacular on a clear day and there is a café up at the top, so you can raise a glass and toast all the Highland majesty that lies at your feet.

The Strathspey Steam Railway will chug you through this mountain scenery to Boat of Garten and back again. Keep an eye on the skies because the endangered osprey are nesting in the nearby Loch Garten Osprey Centre.

The whole trip from Blair Castle to Inverness, though not much more than an hour and a half, is mainly freeway driving so I always welcome the sight of the Little Chef (like a Denny's) about halfway. The food is predictable but the restrooms are clean and you can get a cup of tea to go.

Oh, I should mention here that the majority of rental cars don't have cup holders. I know you're shocked but that's the way it is.

Well, from here on out there is no reason not to put the pedal to the metal and drop down into Inverness.

Stirling to Inverness Diversions Hours & Directions

Bannockburn Heritage Centre, Glasgow Road. Open April-Oct 10am–5:30pm and in Mar, Nov and Dec 11am–3pm. Fee $. The battlefield is open daily and is free for the walking.

Stirling Castle, Upper Castle Hill. Open year round. April-Sept daily 9:30am–6pm, Oct-Mar daily 9:30am–5pm. Fee $$$.

Regimental Museum of the Argyll and Sutherland Highlanders, located within the castle. Open Mon-Sat 10am-5:45pm and Sun 11am–4:45pm. Free.

Valley Cemetery behind the Church of the Holy Rude.

Argyll's Lodging, Castle Wynd. Just across the street from the Church of the Holy Rude. Open same hours as the castle and they share one admission fee.

The Church of The Holy Rude, Saint John Street. May-Sept daily 10am–5pm. Closed Oct-April. Free.

Gleneagles Golf Course and Hotel on the A824 and A823 about a mile and a half from Auchterader. Excellent bus and train service throughout the day from Edinburgh, Perth and Glasgow. See the section on golf courses for information on the 4 courses here.

Jackie Stewart (of Formula One racing fame) School of Shooting and Fishing, 4x4 Off Road Course and the Equestrian Centre, all located on the Gleneagles Estate. You can either get information about these venues by calling the hotel or the Visitors Centre in Auchterarder Ph. 176.466.3450.

Drummond Castle Gardens on the A822 3 miles south of Crieff. Open daily Easter thru Oct 2pm–6pm. Fee $$.

Glenturret Distillery, Hwy A85, Glenturret. Open Mar-Dec Mon-Sat 9:30am–6pm, Sun 12am–6pm; Feb Mon-Sat 11:30am–4pm, Sun 12 – 4. Closed January. Fee $$. Tours, restaurant, and gift shop.

Wildlife and Highland Cattle Centre is 4 miles west and south of Crieff in Comrie just off the B827. Open year round 10am til dusk every day. Visit Chewy, the MacIntosh Toffee mascot, and her calf. Fee $$.

Crieff Visitor Center, Buchan Thistle Pottery and Perthshire Paperweights, Muthill Road, Crieff. Restaurant, play area and garden centre. Open year round. Stuart Crystal, Muthill Road, Crieff directly across the street from Buchan Pottery and Perthshire Paperweights. Open year round. Oct-May, Mon-Sat 10am–5pm, and Sun 11am– 5pm. June-Sept, Mon-Sun 10am–6pm. Falconry display three times a day from April thru Oct.

Strathern Gallery, 32 West High St., Crieff.

Pitlochry Festival Theatre, Foss Road, Pitlochry, Ph. 179.647.2680, www.pitlochry.org.uk or e-mail them at boxoffice@pitlochry.org.uk.

Blair Castle is located in Blair Atholl just north of Pitlochry on the A9. Watch for the sign. The Blair Atholl railway station is 1/2 mile from the castle. Open daily Mon-Sun 10am–6pm. Fee $$$. Beautiful grounds for walking and a picnic, licensed restaurant, and pony trekking can be arranged.

Clan MacPherson House Museum, Clan House, Main St., Newtonmore on the A86. Open April-Oct, Mon-Sat 10am–5pm, Sun 2:30pm–5pm. Free but donations accepted. Small gift shop.

Highland Folklife Museum, Aultlarie, Newtonmore. Open May-Oct but call for times. Note the "call for times" - there is no phone number given by The Scottish Tourist Board. Hmmmm. Fee $.

Highland Folklife Museum, Duke St., Kingussie. Open April-Oct, Mon-Sat 10am-6pm, Sun 2pm–6pm; Nov-March weekdays only 10am–3pm. Fee $.

Aviemore on the major motorway - A9. 12 trains a day travel through Aviemore on their way to or from Inverness so access is great. Highlands of Scotland Tourist Office, Aviemore Branch on Grampian Road, Ph. 147.981.0363 will have current room availability, weather conditions and skiing reports.

Cairngorm Chair Lift, 10 miles east of Aviemore on the B970. Open all year round weather permitting. Fee $$$. There is a café at 3,600 feet. The trip to the top of Cairngorm Mountain takes 25 minutes so dress warmly or carry your sweater or coat for unexpected weather changes.

Strathspey Steam Railway, Aviemore Station, Dalfaber Rd., Aviemore. Daily service Easter to October send for a current schedule. Fee $$$. There are refreshments on the train.

Loch Garten Osprey Centre, Grianan, Tulloch, Nethybridge. Open April-Aug, daily 10am–6pm. You can drive here or take a bus but the easiest is to visit while on your steam railway trip. Telescopes, binoculars and TV cameras permit direct viewing. Fee $.

~9~

The Northeast - The Grampian Region

The Golf Courses:

This part of Scotland is a golf course. There are over 50 courses spread throughout the Grampian region from **Nairn**, up near Inverness, to the **Royal Aberdeen Golf Club (Balgownie)** in Aberdeen. Others of note: **Braemar, Peterhead** and **Fraserburgh**. So if you golf or want to get that golfer out of your hair - this is your chance!

What is a Grampian?

The Grampian actually sounds like the elusive creature we hunted on rainy, summer camp days, but never found. Here in the northeast of Scotland you can find the Grampians in all their glory. The name may not be familiar, but I'm sure every one of us has seen a picture of the kilted Royal Family frolicking at Balmoral Castle, which is in the very heart of the Grampian Mountains.

With its fertile soil and riches from the sea the Grampian region has always been prosperous. Over the ages, this prosperity has lured many to settle comfortably and that continues today with the newly found North Sea Oil just off the coast.

What I like most about this part of Scotland is the downright fun available around every corner. Besides the wealth of golf courses, the region boasts over half of the whiskey distilleries in Scotland along with 70 stately homes and castles.

The tourist agencies have coordinated their efforts and come up with four very unique "Trails" to help you get the most out of your time in the Grampians without floundering blindly around the countryside. The trails are well marked and the attractions have their own signage. For a little variety in your tour, I suggest picking up the brochures for all four of the "Trails" and see where they intersect. A wee dram on the Whiskey Trail certainly may be a welcome relief after three or four stops on the Castle Trail. So let's hit the "Trails"!

The Castle Trail

If you came to Scotland to see castles and stately homes, then the Grampian Region is for you. The beautiful, rolling farmland is literally dotted with them. The National Trust has put together six of their castles and three stately homes, forming a scheme called, appropriately, "Castle Trail". It has an excellent brochure and distinctive blue and white road signage. You can drive the well marked trail, or take a guided tour of the homes that will leave you gasping at a life unknown even to Martha Stewart and a new found respect for the maids and butlers of this world.

These homes are exquisite. Nearly all of them are lived in and play a part in the area's active farming tradition. Every stop has just a little something different to offer visitors above and beyond the ancestral paintings and gilded furniture, and there is always a surprise or two. A few stops along the trail are:

Haddo House:

The working estate of the Gordon Earls of Aberdeen, Haddo House, is an elegant Palladian home set in 180 acres of parkland. The estate supports the Haddo House Choral and Operatic Society which brings performing artists of international repute to its custom-built recital hall.

Duff House:

Designed by William Adam in 1735, Duff House, a Baroque masterpiece, is restored to its former glory and houses major works of art from the National Gallery of Scotland.

<u>Fyvie Castle:</u>

Five glistening towers, each bearing the name of one of its five former owners, crown this Scottish baronial testimonial to remodeling.

<u>Kildrummy Castle:</u>

A 13th Century ruin, rebuilt and ruined, rebuilt and ruined until in 1715, when it was ruined and dismantled. Its last occupant, Bobbing John, went bob, bob, bobbing along to a new home in a subdivision.

Of course, as you travel this part of the country you will be lured off the trail by other public and privately held castles and houses, but never fear, you will not be disappointed by whatever you find at the end of the formal drive.

The Macpherson-Grants will warmly welcome you at <u>Ballindaloch Castle</u> where they have lived continuously since 1546. Can you imagine the garage sale if they moved? Once you see this spread, you'll understand there is not much chance of that ever happening. The stop here at Ballindaloch would not be complete without sampling the local malt whiskey and that leads us directly on to another trail.

The Malt Whiskey Trail

In this region the River Spey's cold, clear and peaty water has been the main ingredient in Scotland's largest selling product - Scotch Whiskey. Seven Speyside distilleries and a cooperage have banded (a cooper's joke) together to welcome guests, instruct them in the art of malt whiskey, and the reverential task of sipping. These seven whiskies are prized for unique tastes to go along with their histories and architecture.

Glenlivet Distillery and Visitors Centre near Tomintoul is the oldest licensed distillery in the north of Scotland and its facility is state of the art. Glenlivet is the largest selling malt whiskey in the United States and the most delicate of the Speyside malt whiskeys, perfect for the beginner if you've never had a single malt before.

Besides the 7 distilleries on the "Trail" you'll find over 40 others in the Grampian Region each producing a distinct flavor of its own. Each distillery also has a look of its own - from the ancient traditional architecture that resembles a pagoda to the modern, utilitarian, metal sided box.

The Malt Whiskey Trail is best traveled carefully by car. Remember this golden brew can be as deadly as delicious. Guided tours and bus service are available during the summer months.

The Fishing Heritage Trail

If your hotel or B&B has offered you the opportunity to have kippers for breakfast, don't pass them up. After all, every Jane Austen character and the *Brideshead* inhabitants seemed to relish kippers with their eggs. You may need a stiff upper lip and a strong cup of tea to get this preserved fish down but you're here for the experience aren't you? If you are still reluctant, ask for a wee taste to heartily fortify you for the trip to the Herring Coast and The Fishing Heritage Trail.

Once the coastline north of Aberdeen was awash in herring, a slithering, wriggling catch that supported huge fleets of fishing boats that crowded into every sheltering harbor. The herring fishery followed in the wake and demise of an active North Sea whaling fleet. The tradition continues today with the busiest fishing port in Europe located in Peterhead (40 miles north of Aberdeen). Peterhead (pronounced Peterheed) is a charming pink granite town that hosts a fleet of colorfully painted boats which at one time could be seen in every fishing village.

Sadly times have changed and only remnants of the huge fishing industry still exist. The memories of Scotland's harsh but lasting romance with the sea can be relived along this "Trail". Every town with a harbor has preserved some part of its proud maritime history whether it be whaling, herring, or now, the oil. You can drop down precipitous slopes to wee collections of homes and sheltering walled harbors to experience what it was like in these extremely isolated and hard working communities.

Pennan

One of these cliff bottom villages is Pennan whose main claim to lasting fame is the movie *Local Hero*. I highly recommend that you rent this film, before your trip to Scotland, for a taste of what village life is all about. Because of the film, Pennan's public telephone booth, one of the stars, is now a National Landmark. The last time I saw that red phone box, the surf was crashing over it and onto the houses on the other side of the road. Did I mention there is one street to this village, buildings only on one side and they face directly out to sea? There are no services other than The Pennan Inn which is across the road from the phone box.

The Pennan Inn (Pennan, Fraserburgh, AB43 6JB, Ph. 134.656.1201, Fax 134.656.1437) is built directly into the cliff and when you are shown up the stairs to your room, the fire escape route is pointed out. If, God forbid, evacuation is necessary you may have to enter another guest's room and climb out the window onto the steep cliff road where you'll probably be hit by the fire truck coming down the hill. The Inn is not a bargain, it isn't luxe and the cuisine isn't haute or nouvelle. Just see the movie and then make your reservations.

The Stone Circle Trail

Ancient peoples have lived, prospered, fought and died here leaving a legacy of stone circles, hill forts and Pictish stone symbols - very interesting if you are into it or a weird and wonderful stop if you're not. You can make up your own mind and here are a few suggested stops:

Mither Tap, - an Iron Age hillfort near Chapel of Garioch.

Loanhead of Daviout Stone Circle, by Inverurie - 4000 years old. Golly, and it's on your way to Fyvie Castle.

Maiden Stone and the Harlaw Monument, near Inverurie. The Harlaw Monument commemorates a battle in 1411 to save Aberdeen from Donald, Lord of the Isles, and the Maiden Stone is a red granite Pictish symbol stone from the 9th century. The Picts had an ongoing battle with the Romans along the borders of Scotland, and that interaction must have been where some Pictish guy saw his first elephant and went home to commemorate it on this stone. I say! Let's have lunch at Fyvie Castle.

Food - Baxter's

Keep your eyes open for the unusual. Baxter's of Fochabers has a huge visitor center filled with their products and other fine Scottish foodstuffs. I can buy Baxter's in a grocery store not far from my home but I've never seen pheasant soup or bramble jam. Baxter's participates in The Taste of Scotland program that you will see advertised all over the country in hotels, fancy restaurants and specialty shops. You will discover some very unusual things on their shelves along with the ordinary, everyday fare. The visitor center offers factory tours, a museum, an excellent and busy restaurant besides a superb kitchen shop.

"Trail" Diversions –

Hours & Directions

Brochures are available from the Aberdeen & Grampian Tourist Board, 27 Albyn Place, Aberdeen AB10 1YL, or www.agtb.org.

The Castle Trail - 6 castles and 3 historic houses owned by The National Trust for Scotland. The trail covers 150 miles and is marked by blue and white signage.

Haddo House, 19 miles north of Aberdeen in Ellon. Just off the B999. Open Easter – Sept, daily 1:30pm–5:30pm and weekends only in Oct. Garden open daily 9:30am–sunset. Fee $$. Bus service from Aberdeen. Beautiful modern restaurant.

Haddo House Choral & Operatic Society. Contact: Haddo House, NTS, Ellon, Aberdeenshire for schedule of events.

Duff House, between Banff and MacDuff, 47 miles north of Aberdeen. Open all year 10am-5pm but only Thurs-Sun between Oct-Mar. Fee $.

Fyvie Castle, 25 miles northwest of Aberdeen and 1 mile from Fyvie Village Bus Station, just off the A947. Open daily Jun-Aug, 11am-5:30pm. Hours shorter in Spring and Fall. Closed Nov-Mar. Fee $$$.

Kildrummy Castle, 10 miles southwest of Alford on the A97. Local bus service from Aberdeen. Open April-Sept, Daily 9:30am-6:30pm. Fee $.

Ballindaloch Castle, Near Aberlour on the A95, 13 miles northeast of Grantown-on-Spey. Open Easter-Sept, Daily 10am-5pm. Fee $$$.

The Malt Whiskey Trail, most participants are open year round with limited hours Nov-April. Best to get the brochure for current hours.

Glenlivet Distillery & Visitors Centre, Ballindalloch, Banff, 10 miles north of Tomintoul. Open Mid-Mar-Oct, Mon-Sat 10am-4pm, Sun 12:30pm-4pm. July and Aug til 6pm. Fee $.

Do not confuse the Distillery with the Royal Estate of Glenlivet.

The Fishing Heritage Trail, also known as the Coastal Trail. 150 miles of seaside adventure. Well signed with white and brown signs.

The Stone Circle Trail, 18 ancient sites from stone circles to hill forts. There are usually no facilities but the price is right. Free.

Mither Tap, southwest of Chapel of Garioch. Visitor Center on the road and the hill fort is an uphill walk. Free.

Loanhead of Daviot Stone Circle is 5 miles north of Inverurie off the B9001. Just north of Daviot. Free.

Maiden Stone, near Chapel of Garioch, 4.5 miles northwest of Inverurie. Just off the A96. Stone stands besides the road. Free.

Harlaw Monument, leaving Inverurie going north on A96 look to your right for the tower on the hill. Free.

Baxter's of Fochabers, just west of Fochabers on the A96. Museum, retail, and restaurant open daily 9am-5:30pm. Factory tours on weekdays only with limited hours.

We've done enough trail ride'n today pardner, so let's head for Aberdeen.

Aberdeen –

The Texas of the North

If you discovered oil in your backyard would you call a golfer? I know that nice golfer, Arnold Palmer, was weaned on Pennzoil but I'd want a real oilman. So when the North Sea was about to give up its first drop of "black gold," the call went out for Texas Oilmen. Spurs didn't jingle jangle as these Texas Oilmen strode into town, but they did bring the cowboy boots and hats and that larger than life attitude of John Wayne. Years later, the oilmen are still there and that drawl doesn't even turn a head.

The North Sea oil has added to the prosperity of the Grampian Region and given Aberdeen, the region's largest city, a cosmopolitan feeling. Ferries coming and going to Scandinavia, an active seaport, and two large universities make Aberdeen a Mecca for ethnic restaurants and fascinating little shops.

The City itself has a very cohesive look about it, for all of its buildings are made out of sparkling, local, grey granite that twinkles at sunset. The nickname "Granite City" is running neck and neck with "Flower of Scotland" in honor of Aberdeen's winning the Beautiful Britain in Bloom competition 10 times. I'm sure you can imagine the parks and public places ablaze in summer with every conceivable herbaceous border perennial and lavishly placed annuals.

If you are a gardener these wonderful gardens are not to be missed:

Pitmedden Gardens (14 miles north of Aberdeen) is a 17th Century Great Garden recreated by the National Trust of Scotland. Highlights of the garden are "thunder houses," rare in Scotland, intricate floral patterned beds, woodland walks and the Museum of Farming Life.

Cruickshank Botanic Garden is right in the heart of Aberdeen and has a unique collection of rock and alpine plants.

Duthie Park and Winter Garden offers year round entertainments. The Winter Garden is Europe's largest indoor garden and there is a Victorian bandstand for summer days. Do not miss the "Rose Mound" which evidences Aberdeen's claim to have 2.5 million rose bushes throughout the city.

Museums Of Note In Aberdeen

Provost Skene's House - A 16th Century townhouse restored to period splendor is right in the center of the town. This is not a huge and glamorous house by "Country House" standards but it was the criteria to which the prosperous politician or merchant of the day aspired.

The Aberdeen Art Gallery is a very open and bright building with a more modern feel than "old worldly" mainly because the collection is from Impressionist, Victorian and 20th Century artists. The "Glasgow School" is given a fine showing here too.

One surprise I particularly enjoyed was a solitary "Costume of the Month" display case standing in a prominent and well-lit spot. Inside the case was a local woman's dress displayed as art. There was a detailed description of the "day" which was exquisitely made and a history of its owner. What a nice idea!

In the basement, the cafeteria is more bistro than the customary tearoom and worthy of a rest stop.

For a more gruesome experience see the Tolbooth Museum on Castle Street. Descend to the cells where witches, highwaymen and common debtors were held. This building hasn't been altered since its construction in 1617. You can also learn about local government but implements of torture are ever so much more interesting.

Aberdeen's many really old buildings may leave you thirsting for a smidgen of modernity, so the Glover House may be just what the doctor ordered. Restored to its Victorian glory (well, it is more modern than 1617), Glover House was built by Thomas Blake Glover who introduced modern coal mining and shipbuilding to the Japanese in the 19th Century. As strange as it may seem, he has been called "The Father of the Japanese Navy". You'll see many Asian influences in the splendid clutter of Victorian home life.

The Aberdeen Maritime Museum is housed in three joined buildings. A modern glass and steel reception/shop area, the old Trinity Church, and Provost Ross's House which was built in 1593, house a fine collection of paintings depicting maritime life and multi-media displays that take you from clipper ships to North Sea oil exploration.

Aberdeen is blessed with two miles of sandy beachfront and a lovely esplanade for strolling. Several seaside amusement/leisure centers and also a ballroom can be found along the beach. If you are more adventurous, how about surfing in the North Sea with the <u>Aberdeen Surfing Club</u>? Virrrrrr! Or how about the <u>Sail Training Association</u> for adventure on the high seas?

Prowling around the dock area you'll find the fish market is already closed if you get there after 8am. The action starts at dawn. The old fishing village of <u>Footdee</u> (Fittie) is at the entrance of the harbor and a delightful starting point for walking the Esplanade.

If you weren't bitten by the Robert Burns Poetry Bug maybe you were infected by the more rare Lord Byron Virus and would like to see where Byron trod as a youth. The <u>Brig o' Balgownie</u> has bridged the River Don since 1329 and was old when Byron walked over it and peered down into his "pool of bewitchment" in the 1700s. You can still walk this bridge today and gaze down at his source of inspiration.

Aberdeen is great for shopping with several large malls and a gracious old department store or two. You leave behind the "chain" type stores the farther from central downtown you get. Most of the really interesting shops I found are around the Art Museum and the Universities. Here the narrow streets are jammed with little coffeehouses and shops selling mirrored Afghan bags and African fabric. This area is very eclectic and a beehive of activity.

Lodging In Aberdeen

Aberdeen is a large city and its suburbs stretch way out from its center. You will have no problem in finding the kind of accommodation you are looking for. I came into town from the north and felt like I was at the mercy of the motel. They were everywhere and not at all appealing. My heart and stomach felt bound up seeing the well signed pub/lounge bar on the premises. I could just hear the music and the drunken laughter at 3am. So I got out my trusty bed and breakfast book and stayed in a nice residential area with quiet streets.

Mrs. Price (105 Osborne Pl, Aberdeen AB2 4DD, Ph.122.464.0780) fit my needs perfectly even though she could only rave about her daughter's guest house. So I will pass the Roselynd House on to you (27 Kings Gate, Aberdeen AB15 4EL, Ph. 122.464.0942, Fax 122.463.6435, e-mail roselynd27@aol.com). The Roselynd appears in many of Tourist Board publications and may just live up to Mrs. Price's boasting.

On The Trail of "The Royals"?

If a Royal Family sighting would "make" your trip, then September in Braemar (60 miles west of Aberdeen) may be your best bet.

Queen Victoria built a little summer shack here in 1855 for her beloved Albert and their brood. All of the "Royals" have been coming back to Balmoral Castle for a jolly good romp ever since. The castle is open to the public from late April until early August when the family arrives, so even if the Queen isn't in to recognize you as a long lost cousin, you can get a peek at a <u>real</u> vacation home.

You might spot Queen Elizabeth II behind the wheel of the estate's well used Land Rover, popping down to the village of Aboyne for dogfood, or is it caviar? On Sunday the crowds take to the road to watch the "Royals" troop to Crathie Church just across from the castle gates. And then if all else fails and you still haven't had a glimpse, try the <u>Braemar Highland Games</u> for a full family sighting.

The village of Braemar is 8 miles west of Balmoral Castle and it has the feeling of a mountain resort, sitting up against the eastern slopes of the Cairngorm Mountains. Lively streams cascade down rocky slopes past sturdy granite hunting lodges and hotels. In the "off" season (October through April), you can't imagine this town draws thousands of participants and spectators for the Braemar Highland Gathering. This traditional Highland Games is the largest in Scotland and includes the always popular dancing and piping competitions. The outrageous caber toss shows off just how virile, or foolhardy, a man in a kilt can be. The truly foolhardy man is the one who thinks he can go up against the little woman who won the skillet toss.

The finale of each day of any Highland Games is the massing of the pipe bands. Competition is put aside and the bands march shoulder to shoulder and even a Chang rises to his feet and claims Scots blood.

If you are not here in September, then Braemar Highland Heritage Centre, right in the center of the village, is an excellent spot to learn the history of the Gathering.

This tiny village offers a nice, small selection of accomodation. I've personally stayed in Callater Lodge Hotel (9 Glenshee Rd., Braemar, Ph. 133.974.1275, Fax 133.974.1345) but right next door, you might try Schiehallion House (10 Glenshee Road, Braemar AB35 5YQ, Ph. 133.974.1679).

Braemar offers excellent walking and climbing and fishing can be arranged. Remember those lively mountain streams I mentioned? Braemar's scrappy little golf course offers long poles with wee nets to help you fish out your cherished "lucky ball" because you wouldn't want to lose it before our next stop... St.Andrews.

Grampian Diversions –

Hours & Directions

Pitmedden Gardens are 4 miles north of Aberdeen on the A920 near Ellon. Open May-Sept, daily

10am–5:30pm. Operated and maintained by The National Trust. Fee $$.

Cruickshand Botanic Garden, Old Aberdeen Campus, University of Aberdeen. Bus #20 from the city center. Open year round Mon-Fri 9am–4:30pm and May-Sept, Sat-Sun 2pm–5pm. Free.

Duthie Park and Winter Garden, Duthie Park, Polmuir Rd. Aberdeen. Open daily, Jan-Mar 9:30am–4:30pm, April 9:30am–8pm, May-Sept 9:30am–9pm, Oct-Dec 9:30am–4:30pm. Free. Restaurant and gift shop. Guided tours are available for a fee.

Provost Skene's House, Guestrow, Aberdeen. Open year round, Mon-Sat 10am–5pm and Sunday 1pm–4pm. Fee $. Coffee shop.

Aberdeen Art Gallery, Schoolhill, Aberdeen. Open year round, Mon-Sat 10am–5pm and Sun 2pm–5pm. Free. Gift shop and excellent tearoom.

Tolbooth Museum, Castle St. Aberdeen. Open April-Sep, Mon-Sat 10am–5pm and Sun 12:30pm–3:30pm. Fee $.

Glover House, 79 Balgownie Road, Aberdeen. Open year round, Tues-Sat 1:30pm–4:30pm and Sunday by appointment. Fee $.

The Aberdeen Maritime Museum, Shiprow, Aberdeen. Open year round, Mon-Sat 10am–5pm and Sun 12pm–3pm. Fee $$. Gift shop & restaurant. A major display on the oil industry includes a huge model of an off shore oilrig.

Aberdeen Surfing Club, no one will cough up a phone number so just listen for the cry "Surf's Up!"

Sail Training Association, 41 Springfield Gardens, Aberdeen AB15 7RX.

Footdee, Take Beach Blvd or Waterloo Quay to the Esplanade, turn right and follow along to the very end of the road. It is charming but don't forget these houses are lived in, so be courteous.

Brig o' Balgownie, At Bridge of Don, north of Aberdeen, upstream of the main A92 bridge. Free. You can walk across 24 hours a day. Built in 1320 and repaired in 1607.

Balmoral Castle, Balmoral, Ballater. 8 miles west of Ballater on the A93. Open daily from mid April–July 10am–5pm. Fee $$. If the family is in residence, the Castle is closed. There is a gift shop and a café.

Braemar Highland Games, The Princess Royal and Duke of Fife Memorial Park, Braemar. Ph. 122.428.8825. Always the first Saturday of September. Fee $$. Book early because they always sell out. Do you know how I know they usually sell out? The brochure is printed with the Grandstand Seating marked "Sold Out" and a note that uncovered seating will be sold out before the day of the games. You can probably get "field" tickets near the date.

The games usually finish about 5pm. Light refreshments are available all day and when the last pipe has pipped, it's a mad dash to the pub.

~10~

The Kingdom of Fife, Angus of the Beef and St. Andrews, The Mecca of Golf

The Golf Courses:

St. Andrews Old Course, New Course and Crail Golfing Society

One of my fondest memories is seeing my extremely ill father standing on the rough of the <u>St. Andrew's Golf Club</u>. Only a "once in awhile" golfer, he still gazed in reverence at the course of legends.

The elegant stone clubhouse of the "Royal and Ancient" overlooks this windswept, seaside links where even the greatest golfers have cursed this barren course for centuries. If you have visions of lush fairways and velvet greens, you'll be as surprised as you will be at the siting of the course. You can literally walk right across the street from the main town and be on the course. Tiger

Woods could probably play the course from the front steps of one of St. Andrews University's lecture halls or perhaps his hotel lobby.

If you have finagled this trip by buttering up an "old duffer", if you actually play, or if "Why yes, I've played St. Andrews" would be a conversation magnet at the next office Christmas party, you should call the nice folks at the Golf Information Centre because they can arrange tee times *and* lessons.

St. Andrews

If you have no interest at all in golf, you can use this line: "Why yes, I've played IN St. Andrews". You'll get the same instant attention because anyone who plays golf will only actually hear "St. Andrews" and you will be telling the truth, for there is lots of playing to be had in St. Andrews.

St. Andrews University is as old and more ancient than the "Royal and Ancient". Scholars have flocked here since 1411 and they still come in all seasons. In the summer months the University offers 2-week courses and inexpensive lodging that is a fun way to become a part of the community. While taking a course on Scottish Place Names, Scottish Art Since 1800, or The Architecture of Charles Rennie Mackintosh, your fellow classmates will become your pals in the evenings and you'll find you have a hoot drinking in student haunts and discovering great old used book stores, just like you did, or wished you did 20, 30, 40 or 50 years ago.

You may be lucky enough to make a "Royal" sighting in and around the town now that Prince William has enrolled. Just look for the swooning maidens and papparazzi and I'm sure you'll find "Wills".

Without ever venturing out of St. Andrews, you can find a complex of ruins – St. Andrews Castle, Cathedral and St. Rules Tower or you can see the exterior of the home where Mary Queen of Scots slept in the 1500's. The home is now St. Leonard's College Library.

The wynds, alleys and lanes are all worth poking around while in St. Andrews. Pop through the gate at Louden's Close and you'll find yourself in a medieval arrangement where several houses share one entrance, and a grassy patch where once vegetables grew and a cow or two grazed.

The Witches Tour is a unique change of pace, as is The Sea Life Centre where you can watch penguins and sea lions just steps from the Royal and Ancient's Clubhouse door. The British Golf Museum is also just across the street from the clubhouse. All you need for these adventures are a good pair of walking shoes.

Touring companies and public transportation, another plus in a university town, offer you the opportunity to climb on a bus and visit the surrounding countryside of Fife and Angus. Fife Scottish, the regional bus company, can offer up a myriad of tours during the summer months. For extremely reasonable prices, they will show you the sights going as far afield as Oban and Ft. William on the West Coast, the border towns in the south with their glorious woollens or a sail on Loch Lomond's romantic waters.

Crail

One of my favorite villages, Crail, is a close-by gem, available on the ordinary bus routes. Sparkling white buildings, a protected harbor, fresh-off-the-boat lobster on the quay, and a pottery on the hill are only some of the joys you can ferret out without a guide. Drawing and painting classes are available in the village, and your camera cannot take a bad picture here. I'll guarantee it.

One of the good things about memories is they are so easily jogged. So if you are a calendar junkie (and what great souvenirs they make), Crail will pop up at least every other year with a month of its own on most Scottish scenic calendars.

World War II is still remembered here with old airfields dotting the landscape (some with museums in the original hangars). A really kitschy, tourist joint - The Secret Bunker is a true relic of the Cold War years. If worse came to worst and Kruschev had moved into a London townhouse or dropped "The Bomb", the government would have been saved. The bunker, entered through a small farmhouse, is hidden 100 feet down way out in the rolling farmland but, like any good old tourist joint it is well signed and advertised. Now, with the demise of the Cold War the bunker is outfitted with destination necessities – café, cinema with dual screens and a gift shop.

Castles and houses of the Fife and Angus region have some pretty Royal links themselves.

Falkland Palace, the hunting lodge of the Stuart monarchs, probably saw some pretty fancily dressed hunting parties, and my Minnesota guy relatives would have to clean up their hunting antics for an invitation here.

If you are a tennis player, you might be interested in seeing the Royal Tennis Court, which was the first in Britain and built in 1539. I'm sure Nike did not supply the sporting ruffles and jewels.

Glamis Castle, the late Queen Mum's birthplace, is still a much loved family home, even with tour groups marching through the living room. The living room reminds me just how much this home is like yours and mine (work with me on this). You know, when your little Eddie makes you a coffee table in wood shop, you just push something out of the way and plunk it down in a place of honor. Well, Glamis' living room has a wig powdering alcove (you never know when that fashion will come around again), and a gorgeous, modern screen made by Queen Elizabeth's nephew and world renowned cabinet maker, Viscount Lindley. The mix of the old and new is really charming and you can imagine the family gathering for drinks before pot roast dinner served in the truly regal, red dining room.

Not far from Glamis is a lovely little town called Brechin. I think I like it because it is built on a hillside. The little shops and houses hug the streets and climb the hill in such a cute little way. The cathedral with the Irish Round Tower is also unique. What I think I like most about Brechin is the fact that I met the most charming gentleman in his frame shop on Swan Street. Mr. Drahony graciously offered me tea and I learned how his Polish accent came to be in Brechin. WWII displaced him and he found the people to be so warmhearted, he never left. I'm sure the ladies of the town wouldn't let him go! He also showed me the watercolors he does for his own satisfaction. They were exquisite, colorful garden scenes and he had never sold even one. Now, he's one of the reasons I travel.

If you've been enchanted by the pictures of steam railway trains then Brechin offers itself as the terminus of the Caledonian Steam Railway.

The Fife and Angus countryside is gentle enough for walks and biking and, except for serious signs in parks warning crazed golfing nuts to take their practice balls and go home, the natives are extremely friendly.

Regular train service to and from Edinburgh, Aberdeen, and Inverness easily opens the country to the "carless". The train stops 4 miles outside of St. Andrews but there is excellent bus service between the train and the town. The truly adventurous can make it all the way north to Thurso or to Kyle of Lochalsh in the northwest where a short but exciting ferry trip can take you to the Isle of Skye. The train takes you through truly spectacular scenery without much effort on your part. Maybe the opening of your snack bag and ordering of a coffee will be the most taxing part of the journey?

I've found some of my best afternoons have been spent in tiny little towns with a pub, a B&B, a grocery, and not much else. These unassuming little spots along the road have very interesting antique shops and bookstores that are catering to the locals rather than the tourists, and what a joy they are. The clerks are usually the owners and they are filled with knowledge about their products and the local area. I bought a great old print in what appeared to be the front room of a home. Lunch was cooking somewhere in the back of the house, but a cup of tea was offered and the owner and I chatted about her finds.

Lodging In St. Andrews

For some reason the hotels of St. Andrews don't hold much interest for me. They appear to be just ho-hum hotels, unless it is your fondest dream to wake up in a room with a view out onto St. Andrews' Old Course. I can highly recommend two bed and breakfasts, right in town, that have taken grand care of me.

The B&B I have favored in St. Andrews has been Deveron House (64 North Street, St. Andrews KY16 9AH, Ph. 133.447.3513), right across the street from the University. The location is perfect and it is always busy so you'd best think about reservations as soon as possible. The owners have lovingly restored the building and my third floor attic room was exquisitely appointed – even pink roses on the tissues. You don't need a college degree in plumbing to run the ensuite bath and the lighting was great for reading all the brochures that I'd collected during the day. The biggest surprise in this fairly formal house was the breakfast room. I don't know if the sunny yellow walls were so welcoming because I could see it sleeting outside the terrace window or if the combination of pine, tile placemats and sunny yellow just made me feel at home. A well prepared breakfast, served by the landlady who had great suggestions for things to do that day and even an invitation to join them at a lecture at the university that night, made my stay memorable. Did I say that you just have to walk around the corner to be at the main shopping street?

My newest favorite place to stay is just around the corner from the golf course. The Brownlees (7 Murray Place, St. Andrews, KY16 9AP, Ph. 133.447.3868), though not as grandly decorated as Deveron House, was extremely comfortable and within two blocks of shopping, the cinema, and restaurants.

I may have been unfair in telling you that Brownlees was not as grandly decorated as the Deveron because the landlords were very proud to tell me that they were in their first week of operation. They had taken their retirement fund and the plunge into their dream of owning a B&B. If the place hasn't turned into an episode of *Faulty Towers*, it may be grander than Deveron House.

Restaurants And Evenings Out In St. Andrews

St. Andrews is a compact little city with a wide range of food choices. As you might expect, there are some pretty swanky restaurants for the affluent golf crowd but there are many, many median and budget priced places that attract the University and town crowd. Great coffee shops, little cafes, French bistros, and rollicking pubs can be found easily. One day I found myself in a beautiful bakery, and when the sugar high from just the smell of the place wore off, I discovered I'd bought enough pastry for the next 3 days. Well I TOLD myself it would take 3 days to eat it.

Because the University and the golf course are right in town, the streets are seldom empty. There are always folks coming and going and I've never felt unsafe walking back to my accommodation, even late at night.

St. Andrews Diversions – Hours & Directions

Whether or not you are with a golfer, St. Andrews has a wealth of pluses for the "golf widow" on the loose.

Golf Information Centre, The Links, St. Andrews. Ph. 133.447.5757.

St. Andrews University Holidays, 66 North St., St. Andrews. Ph. 133.446.2202 for their brochure.

St. Andrews Castle, The Scores, St. Andrews. Open April-Sept, daily 9:30am–6:30pm, Oct-Mar, Mon-Sat 9:30am–4:30pm and Sun 2am–4:30pm. Fee $.

St. Andrews Cathedral and St. Rules Tower, The Scores, St. Andrews. Open the same hours as the Castle. Fee $. The view from the top of the tower is absolutely fabulous!

Witches Tour, check at the Tourist Office on Market Street to see if it will be running the night you want to go.

The Sea Life Centre, The Scores, St. Andrews. Open year round. The hours are daily 10am–6pm but usually longer during the summer months. Fee $$.

British Golf Museum, Bruce Embankment, St. Andrews KY16 9AB. Open year round. Easter-Oct, daily 9:30am–5:30pm. Nov-Mar, 11am–3pm (closed on Tue. and Wed.) Fee $$.

Fife Scottish Omnibuses, Kingdom Centre, Glenrothes, Ph. 159.261.0686. Regular scheduled trips and special tours available.

The Secret Bunker, The address even seems to be a secret, but I'll tell you... Underground Nuclear Command Centre, Crown Buildings (near St. Andrews), Fife KY16 8QH, Ph. 133.331.0301. Fee $$$. On the cryptic map they supply, it appears to be at the convergence of the B9131 and the B940, but the way should be marked with secret brown thistle signs. Good luck! If you decide to chance the directions then be warned, they are only open, April thru Oct 10am–5pm.

Falkland Palace, Garden, and Old Burgh, Falkland, Cupar, Fife. The palace and garden are open April thru Oct, Mon-Sat 11am–5:30pm and Sun 1:30am–5:30pm. During the months of June and Aug the opening hour is 10am Mon–Sat. Fee $$. If you want to see the Old Burgh, you must make an appointment (Ph. 133.785.7397).

Glamis Castle, 6 miles west of Forfar on the A94. Open daily April thru Nov. April-Oct, 10:30am–5:30pm. July and Aug, opening at 10am. November closing time is 4pm. Fee $$$. Excellent restaurant and a picnic ground with a small shop to supply what you've forgotten. Classy little gift shop and a play park for the kids. This is a well thought out operation and the house is superb.

Caledonian Railway, The Station, 2 Park Road, Brechin, Ph. 156.137.7760. The 4-mile railway is open on

Easter, May thru Sept., and in Dec. on Sundays only. Fee $$. I'd call for scheduled times. Charming Victorian train and stations. The restaurant at the Brechin station is in an old dining car.

Now if you can break away from the charming countryside around St. Andrews, I'm ready to get into Edinburgh.

~11~

Edinburgh, The Capital City

The Golf Courses:

Muirfield, Craigmillar Park and Prestonfield

The skirling pipes, swishing kilts, a legendary, romantic Queen, and castled sunsets are here, and everything else Scottish you've ever dreamed about: medieval houses and alleyways, churches redolent with hellfire and brimstone, Victorian department stores, elegant Edwardian suburbs, brilliant gardens, and The Royal Scotsman train. If that's not enough, how about an extinct volcano or two?

What more can I say? Well... costumed actors and miles of TV/movie power cable, a main shopping street (Princes Street not Princess Street) with one of the outstanding views in all of Europe, intimate bistros in the University District, wood panelled/stained glassed pubs filled with hardy dot.com geeks and tweedy working guys, and ice-cream cones with a chocolate stick all can be added to the list.

Neither rain nor shine (usually both every day) nor gusty North Sea breezes can ruin Edinburgh. This is an enchanted place that has capitalized on its romantic history. When Mary, Queen of Scots pointed her little French slipper and lowered her wee, infant son, James, out the castle window and out of harms way the legend spinners took note.

Romance and Edinburgh have been forever linked by the lingering presence of Mary Queen of Scots. Born the daughter of James IV and Mary de Guise during a turbulent time of violence and short lives, Mary became the seventh Stewart monarch just 6 days after her birth in 1542. With that in mind and as a bellweather of things to come, let's do a fast forward chronicle of her life. Now pay attention!

England's Henry VIII was always looking covetously at Scotland and launched his armies at the borders shortly after Mary's father's death. The infant Mary was sent off to France for her safety and married the Dauphine of France (heir to the throne) at 15. When her father-in-law died, her husband became King of France and she, his Queen. Two years later her husband died, and she returned to Scotland bringing French style, language and dance with her. She promptly married Lord Darnley who turned out to be a creep, and she started hanging out with her secretary, Mr. Rizzo. Poor Rizzo was stabbed right in front of Mary's eyes. Who did it? Maybe we could guess? Then Darnley died. Two months later, Mary married the Earl of Bothwell but not before he, being a protestant, divorced his wife to marry the Catholic Mary. About this time, the rigid, stick-in-the-mud Protestants, led by John Knox, had had their fill of Mary's whirlwind lifestyle and forced her to abdicate at the ripe old age of 24. They packed her off to a castle in Lock Leven where she escaped and tried to flee to France. Her fatal error was throwing herself on the mercy of her English cousin, Elizabeth I, a joyless and jealous spinster, who immediately imprisoned her. For the next 20 years, Mary was kept in a series of fortified homes before Elizabeth ended the problem by lopping off Mary's head in 1587.

What may seem ironic is Mary's son, James VI of Scotland, became James I of England at the death of the childless Elizabeth I, and history has just kept swirling along ever since.

Today this romantic story is heralded in pub signs, civic markers, copies of Mary's jewelry, and even food named for events of that time.

If you need any help filling your days here, you are just plain useless and you might as well drown yourself and save the price of a plane ticket. That said, let's see where I'd recommend you start your visit.

Waverly Station, once a dark and dingy train station, has had an extensive facelift, becoming Waverly Centre. Waverly Centre now encompasses the main train lines from the south (London) and the west (Glasgow), the bus station, a gorgeous shopping mall, food court with restrooms, AND the Scottish Tourist Board office where you can book rooms, tours and entertainment.

I can hear you. You said, "Oh great she's sending me to a train station with a mall." Yes, I did because this is where you will make reservations for a guided tour of the City. I know, I know, it sounds corny but let the professional drive you around the warren of one way streets, and have a guide give you the true scoop as well as the lay of the land. The city rambles a bit, so it is easier to get this overview than trying to find parking and the right city bus, or wearing your feet to nubs. You won't need to traipse the whole Royal Mile, thereby saving time to make your own history.

Let's talk a minute about having a car in the city of Edinburgh. I found driving in Glasgow to be truly confusing because of the scale of the buildings so near the sidewalks, traffic near gridlock, and the lack of signage. In Edinburgh the roads are graciously wide. There is traffic, but signage is adequate to get you to where you are going … eventually. What does make driving in Edinburgh a nightmare is the parking situation. You may be able to drive to the venue you want, but then you'll find yourself circling the neighborhood and nearly ending up where you started, having to walk anyway, or you will pay a king's ransom in a parking garage.

Most parking meters on the street are exact-change-only machines that issue a ticket for you to place on your dashboard. Some neighborhoods look like they are free of meters but don't be fooled. There is probably a machine mid-block. Another trick of the parking warden is the sign that warns you not to park after a certain hour as the spot reverts to a "permit holder only" space and you become a pumpkin. That permit holder probably lives on the street and is only too anxious to call the warden so he or she can park fairly close to home.

If you have just arrived in Edinburgh and are without a car, stay that way until you are ready to leave. The bus system and taxis will work magic for you.

Back at Waverly Centre or in the lobby of your accommodation, you should find a "What's On" type of magazine that has a concise map, current entertainment with show times and good ideas to keep you busy. Remember, many of these magazines write up their advertisers in glowing terms, so also check with your lodging, the gal at the bank, or ask the businessman at the next table what they would recommend as a fun (substitute: interesting, unusual, Scottish, burger, romantic, extravagant or cheap-but-good) place for dinner. You might be surprised with the answers. My folks and I once ate in a very stylish cellar that we would have never found without our B&B landlady's directions.

As I have said before, you would have to be a real loser to be unable to fill in your "to-do list" in this town.

Once again I will say it – a <u>good city tour</u> should be at the top of your list. Choose one that takes you into Edinburgh Castle and Holyrood House/Palace. That way you'll get the full history and dubious details without having to waste precious time fumbling through guidebooks and squinting at too small markers. If something really grabs you, then go back later for a closer inspection.

The city is divided into Old Town and New Town with Princes Street being the dividing line. The population boomed in Georgian times, and the newer section of the town reflects the elegant architecture of that era with many crescents, circles and lovely squares that just didn't fit the crowded, hard scrabble way of life in the medieval Old Town up on the hill.

The Royal Mile

The Royal Mile in Old Town Edinburgh runs from The Castle downhill to Holyrood Palace/House. The street is actually four contiguous streets. This multiple street name custom can only be described as, well I guess, quaint. I suppose they found one too many tourists staggering in circles trying to figure out this system and decided Castlehill, Lawnmarket, High Street and Canongate should be commonly known as The Royal Mile.

You'll find scads and heaps of history along the Royal Mile as well as tartans, tacky stuff, cathedrals and ancient houses where the famous and infamous have lived. Some of my favorites are:

John Knox's House has artifacts on display that were actually used by the dour Reverend Knox during his campaign to bring a strict and stern religion to Scotland. This house gives you a fine example of living in the 1500s.

Gladstone's Land is a refurbished house dating from 1620. After the Knox House, I'm sure you can pick out all the "modern conveniences" that had been developed and put into use here.

St. Giles Cathedral, where you might still get a whiff of protestant brimstone, has the most charming spire that looks like a crown and dates from 1495.

The Scotch Whiskey Centre, The Camera Obscura, Brass Rubbing Centre and at least five museums call this street home. The Museum of Childhood is charming and sometimes the noisiest museum in town. The People's Story examines the lives of ordinary people living in Edinburgh from the 1700s forward.

The Castle, The International Festival, and The Edinburgh Tattoo

Edinburgh Castle, at the West end of the Royal Mile, stands on a great stony outcropping that has hosted residents on the site since the Picts used the naturally fortified position as a refuge in the third and fourth centuries. The Castle was a prominent structure as early as the eleventh century and it still gives you one of the most stunning city vistas to be seen anywhere on earth for my money. The Castle itself isn't particularly beautiful. Actually, it is really more of a garrison than a castle but the setting is breathtaking, as it perches on a steep stone outcropping overlooking the city and Princes Street Gardens.

For over 50 years the parade ground (parking lot) of the Castle has hosted the Edinburgh Military Tattoo. The Tattoo is a lavish pipe and drum extravaganza that attracts over 100,000 spectators each year. Bleachers are erected, bands troop and dancers nimbly spring around swords under an impressive bank of lights and finally when your Scots blood starts to boil, there are fireworks.

The Tattoo is held in late August through early September during the Edinburgh International Festival which is billed as the "World's Largest Arts Festival." The whole town and towns all around, fill tight up to the gunnels with participants and spectators alike, so book **early**.

"The Festival" has been bringing the world to Edinburgh's doorstep since 1947, and you'll find absolutely every taste satisfied. One night you may have to choose from a staggering list that may include live theater, a ballet troupe from New York, a symphony orchestra from the Netherlands, opera from Italy, and once-in-a-lifetime art exhibits or maybe your high school drama department singing and dancing its heart out. Running simultaneously is the Edinburgh Fringe Festival, which was the brainchild of university students who felt their talents were being overlooked. Well, not to be overlooked now, there are as many as 15,000 performances including street theater, alternative music, comedy, traditional Scots music, new plays, poetry, parades and some just crazy foolishness.

If these three events haven't clogged every highway and sidewalk and overbooked every room for miles around then just to make sure the town is as full as possible they've added in: The Edinburgh Jazz Festival, The Edinburgh Book Festival, and The Edinburgh International Film Festival.

Phew! A vacation may be in order after visitng Edinburgh at Festival Time.

Holyrood House or Palace

At the east end of The Royal Mile, <u>Holyrood House,</u> is a true Palace. Queen Elizabeth II and Prince Philip stay here when they are in Edinburgh, and use the same apartments that saw so much intrigue during Mary Queen of Scots reign. We can only imagine the intrigues of today.

Edinburgh's Museums

There are absolutely too many to list but here are my favorites:

<u>Museum of Scotland</u>. Located in the ancient Old Town, this award winning building opened in 1998 and presented a stark, modern face to the six streets that converge at its front door. The imposing, sandy colored, stone building offers design themes reminiscent of the collections inside. Starting in the lower level of the building, you'll be introduced to the land before man (pre 8000 BC) and then proceed up over seven floors, or levels, through time, to a good-humored "current time" exhibit. The displays are not crowded because the items chosen are displayed not only as a bit of historical perfection but as art. Some of the items I wouldn't have looked at in a typical museum setting but here, even ancient farm implements become enthralling.

Next door <u>The Royal Museum</u> offers a more traditional museum setting. The old gracious building is actually connected to the Museum of Scotland and one admission fee covers both. Many unusual displays and changing exhibits make this a lively place frequented by the locals. The day I visited, a queue was forming for a vintage *film noir* festival.

If the weather is dicey this museum duo can easily fill most of a day, and the coffee shop in the Royal Museum was terrific for a quick stop. The Museum of Scotland's Round Tower boasts one of Edinburgh's premier fine dining venues, The Tower, with views to die for from every seat in the house.

Here is an invaluable hint – Do not, I repeat, Do not check your camera because the restaurant's superb views are available from the roof top terraces. If the weather is unusually awful, they close the terraces but I pray that the day you are there, they are open.

While you are out on the terrace look down to find Greyfriars' Kirk. This little church is lovely on its own but the legend of Greyfriars' Bobby is what makes it so special. Bobby was a wee terrier who spent 14 years guarding his master's grave in the churchyard. There is now a lovely little fountain offering dog height drinks in front of a pub aptly named Greyfriars' Bobby Bar. The pub, not a new marketing scheme, has been on this spot since 1722 and is extremely popular.

The National Gallery of Art, located front and center on Princes Street, The National Portrait Gallery (5 blocks from Princes Street) and The National Gallery of Modern Art, just a short taxi or bus ride from Waverly

Center, will pretty much cover everything from classical to the latest strange trend. These three marvelous facilities will have brochures and flyers posted for local arts events throughout the city in case you are wanting to delve deeper into the active art world of Edinburgh.

Musical history is cherished in Edinburgh University's Historic Musical Instrument Collection and The Russell Collection of Early Keyboard Instruments.

Within Ten Miles of Princes Street

The Royal Botanic Garden offers 70 acres of magnificent landscape including Britain's tallest glass Palm House. Their collection of rhododendron is one of the world's finest and an ongoing exploration in Asia is expanding the collection yearly.

The Edinburgh Zoo is a nice change of pace, especially if you have little people along. Everyday at 2pm, from April through September, there is a Penguin Parade featuring the largest penguin colony in Europe. These little tuxedoed creatures will make you laugh until it hurts.

The Royal Observatory not only offers you the chance to use multi-media computers to explore space, but if you have an interest in the heavenly skies, you might want to make arrangements to see one of the largest telescopes in Scotland. The views back at Edinburgh from Blackford Hill are extraordinary too.

The Scottish Mining Museum is an actual Victorian colliery with the pit and hoists and wheelhouses. I didn't go out to the mine because I get the creeps when I think of going underground, but now I've discovered they have computers that take you "virtually" into the mine. Now that is my kind of spelunking.

Craigmillar Castle serves up more Mary Queen of Scots intrigue along with an ancient keep and lushly furnished rooms.

Drive around Arthur's Seat, an extinct volcano in Holyrood Park, and see some of the most extravagant views you'll see of the city.

Edinburgh Crystal Visitor Centre can be reached easily via a free hourly bus from Waverly Bridge just outside Waverly Centre. Besides a countryside jaunt, you'll see the entire manufacturing process from blowing to cutting, and then, enjoy a cup of tea in the restaurant or just shop for bargains. Their Scottish Thistle pattern makes a cherished souvenir whether you take home a suite of wineglasses or a wee dram glass for your pansies.

Butterfly and Insect World, next door to Scotland's largest garden center, allows you to get up close and personal with spectacular tropical butterflies and other exotic insects, all in an indoor rainforest.

Midlothian Ski Centre has manmade slopes for year round schussing. Lessons are available for all experience levels. So why not learn how to snow plow in July? It's warmer than Vermont in February.

The Royal Yacht Britannia, now berthed in Leith, no longer sails the waves, but you can pay for the privilege of seeing how the "Royals" enjoyed themselves on state voyages and romantic honeymoons. We all remember the photos of Charles and Diana waving happily from the deck as they set out on their life of marital bliss.

Edible Choices In Edinburgh

Again, ask for dining suggestions but give a hint as to style or price range. Often when you ask strangers for recommendations they want to give you a great impression of their city. Not a bad thing, but they may recommend a place that is absolutely over-the-top fabulous with prices to match. They have never been there and they might overlook their favorite little place that serves up a veal piccata that melts in the mouth while leaving the wallet intact.

Again, this is a city catering to tourists, so some of the most popular places may just be popular because they are opposite the Burns Monument. When you are looking for a place and have no recommendation, peek around the corner from the closest attraction and you may find a gem without the tourists.

I found the little neighborhood of Grassmarket to have a great selection of ethnic places. The neighborhood is directly under The Castle walls on the Old Town side. One little spot, right on the car park side of the square, that I'm hoping will be there next trip, was Ristorante Gennaro. A lovely Italian family was most anxious to make sure I was happy and comfortable besides being extremely well fed.

High tea is always fun in one of the big, grand old hotels so take advantage of the opportunity. Put on your posh frock, or the closest thing to one, and try the Caledonian Hotel or the Palm Court in the Balmoral Hotel. Both of these grande dames are on Princes Street.

If I could go back today for an elegant dining experience, I'd ask for a table at The Tower in the Museum of Scotland. The sleek modern interior looks out over the Old Town and straight at The Castle. I'd ask for a late sitting so that I would catch the sunset and see The Castle illuminated. An added attraction, if you are there during The Edinburgh Festival, would be nightly fireworks above The Castle.

If you can't bring yourself to sit upright in a restaurant after a full day of touring and shopping, then might I suggest the local fish & chips, pizza take-out, or baked patato shop. If you're lucky, you'll be able to get all three in the same spot and you can mix and match a meal. I love haddock and a big, cheesey, baked spud, my shoes off and the pillows plumped. Yummm! Regroup and go out for a nightcap later.

Lodging In Edinburgh

Hundreds of small hotels and B&Bs are available in and around Edinburgh, but depending on the time of the year, there might as well be none. If you are going at the height of the summer, book a room in advance. If you are going during The Festival weeks (late August - early September) and haven't booked already, you may be in for a shock. So as soon as you have your schedule get on the phone or fax and book.

The Beresford Hotel (32 Coates Gardens, Edinburgh EH12 5LE, Ph. 131.337.0850) is my current "very favoritest" place to stay. Donald and Agnes Mackintosh have worked their fingers to the bone righting a beautiful old row house. When the renovation work began, the house was near death as a seedy 1960's psychodelic décor hotel. The pride displayed here is evident, right down to the lovingly restored plaster moldings. Even though the Beresford is within walking distance of Princes Street, you have the feeling of being in a neighborhood with a lovely, gated park and family homes.

Mrs. Helen Baird offers Bed and Breakfast in her small detached bungalow for the true feeling of an in-home stay, rather than a guest house or small hotel. Mrs. Baird can be reached at Arisaig, 64 Glasgow Road, Edinburgh EH12 8LN or by phone at 131.334.2610.

Like most large cities Edinburgh has its chain hotels including Best Western, Hilton, and Intercontinental. The buildings may be old or new but you will get the same bland service you've come to expect from them.

If you need the country house experience then try Prestonfield House, a Jacobean home designed by the architect of Holyrood House. Lush walled gardens, peacocks and views of Arthur's Seat will fill your dance card to overflowing. Of course your budget may be blown on a night's stay, but hey, it is a country house just a 15 minute drive from Princes Street. Ph. 131.668.3346, Fax 131.668.3976 or e-mail: prestonfield_house@compuserve.com

Shopping In Edinburgh

I won't be bothered to tell you about shopping in Edinburgh. If you can't find what you are looking for, then reconsider my advice about drowning yourself. At least the headlines will be entertaining – "Shopowners Vindicated", "Unused Visa Card Baffles Police", "Sale Racks Bulged Before Mysterious Death".

Get going and look beyond Princes Street.

Edinburgh Diversions –

Hours & Directions

John Knox's House, 43-45 High Street on The Royal Mile. Open year round. Mon-Sat 10am-4:30pm. Fee $.

Gladstone's Land, 477B Lawnmarket on The Royal Mile. Open April thru October. Mon-Sat 10am-5pm; Sun 2pm-5pm. Fee $$.

St. Giles Cathedral, High St. on The Royal Mile. Open year round but closed to sightseers during services.

Hours: Mon-Sat 9am-5pm (7pm in summer); Sun 1pm-5pm. Admission is free but a donation is suggested.

Scotch Whiskey Centre, 354 Castlehill on The Royal Mile. Open daily 9:30am-6-30pm. Fee $$.

The Camera Obscura, Castlehill on The Royal Mile. Open daily 10am-5pm (6pm in summer). Fee $$.

Brass Rubbing Centre, Chalmers Close, 81 High Street, Edinburgh. Just off the Royal Mile opposite the Museum of Childhood. Open March thru October, Mon-Sat 10am-5pm. Free for the watching but charges for making rubbings.

Museum of Childhood, 42 High St. on The Royal Mile. Open year round. Mon–Sat 10am-5pm and during the "Festival", Sun 2pm-5pm. Free.

The People's Story, 163 Canongate on The Royal Mile. Open year round. Mon–Sat 10am-4pm and during August, Sundays 2pm-5pm. Free.

Edinburgh Castle, Castlehill at the west end of The Royal Mile. Open year round. Daily Oct-Mar 9:30am-4:15pm. Apr-Sept 9:30am-5:15pm. Fee $$$.

Edinburgh Military Tattoo, 32 Market St., Edinburgh
EH1 1QB, Ph. 131.225.1188. Tickets and information. Book early.

Edinburgh International Festival, The Hub, Castle Hill, Edinburgh EH1 7ND, Ph. 131.473.2000. Tickets and information. Book early.

Edinburgh Fringe Festival, 180 High St., Edinburgh EH1 1BW, Ph. 131.226.5257. Tickets and information.

Edinburgh Jazz Festival, 116 Cannongate, Ph. 131.557.1642. Tickets and information.

Edinburgh Book Festival, Scottish Book Centre, 137 Dundee St., Ph. 131.228.5444. Note this is not an annual event.

Edinburgh International Film Festival, 88 Lothian Rd., Ph. 131.228.4051. Tickets and information.

Holyrood Palace/House, Canongate at the east end of The Royal Mile. Open Daily unless the Royal Family is in residence. These closures are usually the last 2 weeks in May and 3 varying weeks in June and July. Phone: 131.556.7371. Hours: Mon-Sat 9:30am-4:45pm and Sun 10:30am-4:40pm. Fee $$$.

Museum of Scotland and The Royal Museum, Chambers St. (From the intersection of Lawnmarket and High St on the Royal Mile walk south on Melbourne Place/George IV Bridge about 4 blocks). Hours: Mon-Sat 10am-5pm, Tuesdays until 8pm and Sun noon 'til 5pm. Fee $ for the Museum of Scotland. The Royal Museum is free.

Greyfriars' Kirk, located behind Greyfriars' Bobby Pub, at the intersection of Candlemakers Row and George IV Bridge, is kitty corner from the Museum of Scotland. Open daily (so's the pub at the front gate).

The National Gallery of Art, 2 The Mound (midway on Princes St.) Mon-Sat 10am-5pm and Sun 2pm-5pm. Longer hours during The Festival. Free unless there is a special exhibit.

The National Portrait Gallery, 1 Queen St. (4 blocks north of Princes St. at the west end of the street). Mon-Sat 10am-5pm and Sun noon 'til 5pm. Free unless there is a special exhibit.

The National Gallery of Modern Art, Belford Road. Bus service from the city center or a 15 min. walk from the west end of Princes St. Mon-Sat 10am-5pm and Sun noon 'til 5. Free unless there is a special exhibit.

Edinburgh University's Historic Musical Instrument Collection, Reid Concert Hall, Bisto Square. Ph. 131.650.2423. Open Wed 3pm-5pm and Sat 10:00am-1pm. During The Festival Mon-Fri 2pm-5pm. Free.

The Russell Collection of Early Keyboard Instruments, Niddry St., Cowgate (in the Old Town), Ph. 131.650.2805. Open Wed and Sat 2pm-5pm and during The Festival Mon-Sat 10:30am-12:30pm. Fee $.

The Royal Botanic Garden, 20a Innerleith Row (1 mile north of Princes St.), Ph. 131.552.7171. Opens 9:30am and closes at varying seasonal times (Nov-Jan 4:00pm, Feb-Oct 5:00pm, Mar and Sept 6:00pm, Apr-June 7:00pm, and July–Aug 8:00pm. Free.

Edinburgh Zoo, 134 Corstorphine Road, Edinburgh. 3 miles west of the city center but served by city bus. Open daily, April-Sept, 9am-6pm and Oct-

March 9am-4:30pm. Fee $$$. Besides the hilarious April-Sept Penguin Parade, you can experience the Darwin Maze and white rhinos.

Scottish Agricultural Museum, Ingliston, Newbridge, Midlothian. By the Edinburgh Airport so you can take a city bus directly or an airport bus and a 10 minute walk. Open April-Sept, daily 10am-5pm; Oct-March, Mon-Fri 10am-5pm. Free.

Royal Observatory, Blackford Hill (3 miles south of Princes St.) Ph. 131.668.8405. Open Mon-Sat 10am-5pm and Sun noon 'til 5pm. Fee $.

Scottish Mining Museum, Lady Victoria Colliery, Newtongrange, Midlothian. On the A7, 10 miles south of Edinburgh. Accessible by bus from Edinburgh. Open Feb-Nov 10am–5pm daily. Fee $$. Scotland's finest surviving Victorian colliery and you can visit a virtual coalface.

Craigmillar Castle, Craigmillar Castle Rd. (2.5 miles southeast of Princes St.), Ph. 131.661.4445. Apr-Sept, Mon-Sat 9:30am-6:30pm and Sun 2pm-6:30pm. Oct-Mar, Mon-Wed and Sat 9:30am-6:30pm and Sun 2pm-4:30pm but Thursdays in the morning only and closed Fri. Fee $.

Edinburgh Crystal Visitor Centre, Eastfield, Penicuik 8 miles southwest of Princes St. Free shuttle bus from the Acanthus Café Bar on Waverly Bridge (Apr 1–Oct 1). Free but beware of overheating your Visa Card in the factory shop. Hours year round: Mon-Sat 9am-5pm and Sun 11am-5pm.

Butterfly and Insect World, Dobbies Garden World, Lasswade (near Dalkeith 5 miles south of Edinburgh). Open year round during business hours 9:30am 'til 5:30pm in summer and 10am 'til 5pm in winter. Fee $$.

Midlothian Ski Centre, Hillend, Near Edinburgh just off the A702 at Lothianburn junction. Bus from Edinburgh. Open winter, Mon-Sat 9:30am–9pm, Sun 9:30am–7pm; summer Mon-Fri 9:30am–7pm and weekends 9:30am–9pm. Fee $$ for skiing and a Fee $$ to just ride the chairlift for spectacular views. Lessons for all levels, equipment rental, café, and artificial ski slopes. No wet mittens or soggy boots, guaranteed on a clear summer's day.

The Royal Yacht Britannia, Ocean Drive, Leith (a suburb in north Edinburgh). Pre-booking advised as this is an extremely popular attraction. Ph. 131.555.5566 or tickets are available at the Edinburgh Tattoo Office, 33-34 Market St., Edinburgh. Britannia's hours are usually 9:30am 'til 4:30pm but longer in August and shorter in winter. There is a hefty admission fee ($$$) to keep Britannia afloat.

-12-

The Borders –
From Ewe to Coutour

The Golf Courses:

**Eyemouth, Hawick/Vertish Hill, The Roxburghe
and St. Boswells**

Lush pastoral hills just to the north of England, "The Borders", have long been a fabled land of highwaymen and poachers. This is the area where that great, great, great uncle, the one that most American families seem to have, came from. You know the one - the "blacksheep", who was thrown out of Scotland before he got himself hanged.

To commemorate the violent past of the bands of thieves and marauding armies, Common Ridings are held throughout the Borders in early summer. These Ridings are centerpieces for town celebrations. The local townsmen, dressed in costume, mount their steeds (often rented for the day) and head out into the countryside, much like a posse of the Old West. Drink is often liberally applied before the event to ease resulting saddle sores, so there is much gaiety, even in horrid weather.

Convenient wooded ravines suitable for hiding from the sheriff's men still offer shelter to fishermen and wildlife, but today the only highway robbery may involve the butcher shorting you a sausage or the "widowmaker's" golf partner shaving a point off his game.

Getting to the Borders is not an easy task even though it is anywhere from 20 to 50 miles from Edinburgh. The rail lines now only skirt the area on the east and west. Don't be fooled by the rail brochures that lead you to believe you can take the train into the border towns. That train really only connects with a mildly effective bus system. A car is imperative if you are going to snoop around border towns. The roads are good and not overly busy.

Being so close to Edinburgh may lead you to believe that the amenities of the big city would be readily available here. Sure the Safeway and D.I.Y. (do-it-yourself) stores may give you the impression of a go-get-'em twenty-first century place but don't let that deceive you. You are in the country and the entertainment is homemade. Watch for posters and check the local papers for entertainment. The ladies aid society may be having a fundraising morning coffee where handmade crafts can be purchased. I've bought some of the most precious, knit, baby presents at these local events. Don't feel you are imposing. These are small communities and a new face is always welcome.

This "homemade" entertainment has spawned a great many craft workshops and galleries. The <u>Scottish Borders Council</u> has produced a stylish brochure entitled *Arts & Crafts,* featuring many of them. They may need a copywriter with a little bit more "oomph," but there is nothing slouchy about the up-to-the-minute artists and artisans included in the brochure.

I love coming to The Border Region because the towns, though close together, are completely different in feel. From dour to delightful, these towns also offer the visitor completely different focuses for their existence.

As unique as their specialties, the border towns each also have their own appearance. These towns look like they get the job done. The streets are wide to accommodate shipping of goods or the marketing of animals. The architecture is utilitarian, and from shop to shop the buildings can change style and century like magic. The main street of Peebles is a fine, quirky example of this lack of cohesive town style. Ancient stone buildings share common walls with 1930s cinemas or fluffy Victorians.

All over the Borders older buildings are being restored and given new uses, like Hawick's Drumlanrig's Tower which started its life as an ancient civic building then in the 1930s became the Tower Hotel. This "gracious" hotel, as the guidebooks still describe it, was actually a cold tomb of a place where I never thought I'd get warm again. The hotel has now been transformed into tourist offices, town museum, and council offices and the whole feel of the place has changed. I can't believe the main floor windows are the originals, because today the tourist office just squints in the brightness where I only remember gloom.

The town of Melrose has newfound pride in its long closed railway station that is now a beautiful suite of offices and a very good restaurant.

Frolicking wee lambs still gambol across the fields, bleating and butting in the spring while their mums and dads quietly grow next season's crop of wool. Their products and that of sheep and goats from around the world, will end up in border towns and villages devoted to the manufacture of the world's finest woolens.

Paris runway models are always sporting Clan Tartans, cashmere knits, and investment quality tweeds that look thoroughly modern with each season's passing fancy. Donna Karan, Anne Klein and Ralph Lauren regularly place orders for their "American" looks.

But sadly, as farming has become harder with every year, as it has become world wide, and because of the recent hoof and mouth epidemic, the fields are raising a new cash crop – golf courses. New courses are opening at a steady clip here in the Borders and some of them are very good. This offers the "Golf Widow" a huge opportunity. As tee times are readily available, you can dump the old duffer at any number of courses. Contact the Scottish Borders Tourist Board for their <u>Freedom of the Fairways</u> brochure which offers 3 day (6 rounds) or 5 day (10 rounds) Passports useable at 21 participating courses. Then you're free to hit the mills, factory outlets, and wee shops specializing in each town's specialty.

So what about those town's specialties I've been talking about? Well, let's start right along the border with England. After all, that's why they call this area "The Borders".

Hawick (pronounced Hoyck)

You can go into Hawick and find that woven fabric is a rare commodity but you can get anything from an artist-made, one-of-a-kind sweater to elegant, butter soft, cashmere bathrobes and evening wraps. Hawick <u>is</u> knitting. The yarn is made here, dyed here and knit here. Knitting is often done in centuries old factories, now retrofitted with computer driven machines that do everything from traditional flat or ribbed knits to the multi-colored, multi-yarned sweaters you see in the most exclusive shops.

If you knit, try <u>Jean's</u> a little yarn shop just across from the Leisure Centre in Hawick. This tiny shop looks like an earthquake has sent everything flying onto the floor, but Jean Marsden knows where everything is and she is a wealth of information. She has a treasure trove of patterns and a local clientele that drops in for "a bit of yarn for Fiona's baby girl".

Lodging In Hawick

Kirkland's Hotel (West Stewart Place, Hawick, TD9 8BH.Ph. 145.037.2263) A great old Victorian home that now serves as a gracious hotel and clubby meeting place for the local *hoi palloi*. It has lovely rooms, some with a view over the town and one of the town's lawn bowling clubs. Great casual meals are served in the cosiest of bars and gracious dining in the formal dining room. This is the kind of a place you could meet a lifelong friend.

Elm House Hotel (17 North Bridge Street, Hawick,TD9 9BD. Ph.145.037.2866) This small in-town hotel has your budget in mind.

Oakwood House Bed and Breakfast (Buccleuch Road, Hawick, TD9 0E. Ph. 145.037.2814) A Victorian house with lovely garden.

Shopping In Hawick

Hold onto your wallet -- it's time for cashmere shopping! When it comes to making a cashmere purchase, just remember what you'd charge to comb a goat.

Hawick Cashmere Company, Peter Scott and Valeri Louthan offer some of the finest in knitwear. If you are old enough to remember when every "girl" needed a cashmere sweater or die, then you'll remember the brand name Pringle of Scotland and you can visit this high holy place in Hawick. The cashmeres sold in these establishments are not the Made in Hong Kong, $100.00, Christmas sweaters that quickly loose their shapes, but the wonderful heavy weight cashmere that our mothers and grandmothers bragged about and wore so proudly. No limp "pashmina" here. In fact I think there is a "No pashmina" sign at the Hawick city limits. Prices are at least 20% less than in the department stores and wholesale prices are often the norm.

A lesson in the violent nature of this part of the country is <u>Hermitage Castle</u>, a big, square, windowless ruined pile, now only a reminder of the marauding armies that traveled this route into Scotland. Mary Queen of Scots stayed in Hermitage Castle on her way to see her wounded lover, Lord Bothwell. It must have been true love because this place is gloomy and foreboding. Clan Douglas moved in here in 1320.

<u>Milnholm Cross</u>, four miles south, commemorates one of the lives lost at Hermitage Castle. The cross, erected about 1320, is in the care of The Clan Armstrong Trust that, much to my Scots family's delight, remembers the murder of Alexander Armstrong. Yes, I admit it, I had a long lost Armstrong relative who got himself out of Scotland in the nick of time. If you are an Armstrong, this is your country and there are churches, museums and old coaching inns connected with a very colorful history.

<u>Border Fine Arts Gallery</u> is located in the town of Langholm about 20 miles south east of Hawick. You will find their exquisite animals in every good gift shop in Britain. Farm life is the major theme, so there are sheepdogs, pigs, cows and crafty foxes looking as if they could spring to life. Their china mugs are excellent gifts and reminders of the gorgeous countryside.

Galashiels

Galashiels, to the north of Hawick, is known for woven fabric. When I asked where I might buy yarn, I was told matter-of-factly that "Gala is a weaver's town". Oops! Directions were given to Mrs. Marsden's shop in Hawick. I had obviously committed a grave error.

Weaving is a time-honored tradition in Scotland and in times past, looms could be heard making their unique rhythmic music in homes and cottages throughout the countryside. Today in "Gala," vast computer driven looms whirr with the sound of yards being woven in minutes. The romance may be gone but the beauty remains.

The quintessential fabric of Scotland is the plaid or more properly the Clan Tartan. A great deal of lore has revolved around these treasured family yard goods, and today Clan Tartan is regulated by the Registers at Lyon Court where the patterns are minutely guarded down to each warp and weft yarn. New patterns are introduced every once in awhile and some meet with success. The Princess Diana Tartan was done to honor the memory of a wonderful woman, but it is also a tasteful and wearable addition to the registered tartan repertoire, unlike some older traditional and newer introductions. One big expensive mistake was the U.S. Bi-centennial Tartan - a red, white and blue bout of madness.

Galashiels doesn't offer much in the way of tourist activities but it is the home of <u>Lochcarron of Scotland</u>, one of the most reputable and respected makers of tartan in Scotland. It is located in an old stone mill once powered by the river that flows under and around it. A museum has been added to track the history of weaving in Galashiels and mill tours are available. You'll see what is involved in making intricate and exacting tartans and other gorgeous fabrics that may well end up in a Channel suit.

Lodging In Galashiels

<u>Woodlands House Hotel and Restaurants</u> (Windyknowe Road, Galashiels TD1 1RG. Ph. 189.675.4722) is a let-out-the-stops, blow-the-wad, Gothic Mansion with 3 restaurants, oak paneling, grand staircase and conservatory.

<u>Maplehurst Guest House</u> (Abbotsford Road, Galashiels TD1 3HP, Ph. 189.675.4700) a relatively new house in the overall scheme of things this Edwardian family house is lovely and it sits in its own grounds.

Maplehurst reminds me of the gracious old sorority house you see on university campuses.

Melrose

Idylic is one of the best words to describe a stay here. Gentility oozes out of the pores of this town. The hills have fallen away and gardens and nurseries lure you with their wares. Uniformed children from posh schools live in picture book houses just down the lane from a Roman fortress. Well-equipped golfers and fly fisherfolk dart in and out, on the way to excellent courses and streams.

If you squint you can even avoid the sight of encroaching urban sprawl from Galashiels.

Scotland's most famous author, Sir Walter Scott once frequented Melrose and many references to him are made in and around the town. Melrose Abbey, now only a 14th Century Gothic ruin, was mentioned as best seen "in the pale moonlight" in Scott's poem *The Lay of the Last Minstrel*. The ruins are right in town so a walk for that view is perfect just before bed.

Abbotsford House, Sir Walter's home, is located just outside of Melrose. *Ivanhoe* and *Waverley*, two of his best loved novels, were probably penned here.

True to the era, Abbotsford is built in a highly romantic style of the early nineteenth century. Part poet's monastery, part baronial mansion, Sir Walter stuffed it to the gills with books and bric-a-brac he'd collected. The library contains a collection of 9,000 books. Beautifully paneled, the dining room, where Sir Walter died, has a charming view out to the River Tweed. Scott's ancestors still live here and lovingly take great care of the place.

Scott's View takes you to one of the highest points in Scotland, and the view down onto the River Tweed and its lush valley is magnificent and absolutely free for the viewing. The Eildon Walk, which starts in Melrose, will take you up into the Eildon Hills and Scott's View. The walk takes about an hour and a half, is not difficult, but good walking shoes are advised.

Dryburgh Abbey, Sir Walter's resting-place, is a huge ruin just sitting in a field. No fanfare or hoopla and not much of a building, but your visit is helped along with informative signage. Just across an adjoining field the Dryburgh Hotel, in all of its country house glory, reigns over the abbey ruin. You are truly out in the countryside.

Priorwood Gardens', right next door to Melrose Abbey, *raison d'être* is the growing of flowers that can be preserved. If you've grown tired of plain old dried hydrangea and statice, you'll be pleasantly surprised by what you can easily grow and dry. The National Trust for Scotland maintains the garden.

Teddy Melrose is a museum devoted to the Teddy Bear in Britain and a wonderful stop for clearing one's head of serious history. The museum shop caters to collectors who are tempted mightily with Border Bruins in tartan wear.

The Trimontium Exhibition (Melrose Market Square) chronicles the largest Roman fort in Scotland. Artifacts gleaned from the archaeological dig are well displayed and there is a guided tour of Roman sites around Melrose.

Lodging In Melrose

My personal favorite is Burt's Hotel (Market Square, Melrose TD6 9PN, Ph.189.682.2285). Built in 1722 as a coaching inn, the stairs are narrow, floors squeak and groan, and the ceilings are low. Aside from these appealing amenities, the beds are good andthe dining room cuisine is excellent. The lounge bar offers up great casual meals, lively local conversation, and on a sunny day, the back garden is the perfect place to throw out the touring schedule and sit back with several pints or a bottle of wine.

Dunfermline House Guest House (Buccleuch St., Melrose TD6 9LB, Ph.189.682.2148), right in the town center, overlooks Melrose Abbey and is easy on the budget. No dinners are served but you are within steps of Burt's Hotel.

Dryburgh Abbey Hotel (St. Boswell's TD6 0RQ, Ph. 183.582.2261) is truly regal and another blow to the budget, country-house experience. There is a subdued décor and pasture vistas which include Dryburgh Abbey just next door. Be prepared to dress for dinner (jacket and tie for the men), as you will have to get into the car to find a casual meal. The hotel is right on the River Tweed for your wading or fishing pleasure.

Kelso

Industry has passed up Kelso but that does not mean the town's folks aren't industrious. Horsebreeding and sheep husbandry are labor intensive activities and, the fruits of these labors can be seen at the agricultural fairs and the Kelso Races that are held throughout the year. This town thrives on farming.

Kelso's town fathers are taking great care to see that even new buildings blend in with the very old, picture postcard, Scottish architecture of the place. All roads lead directly to the central square, which offers abundant parking, small town shopping, and a choice of hotels. There are unique craft and antique shops tucked away so it's fun to snoop the quiet streets and lanes.

Floors Castle, within sight of Kelso, is unlike any other castle or stately home in Scotland. Besides being the largest inhabited stately home in Scotland, Floors has turrets and googaws and ornamental pediments that just scream "fairy tale". The Roxburghe family is gracious enough to put aside their daily lives for a few hours so we can see a vital, living piece of history. I was once at Floors when the lady of the house must have been surprised at how time flies. Her open address book and the phone were on the drawing room sofa, amid a pile of mail and personal belongings just like we commoners all seem to generate on a Saturday morning. It was very refreshing to know that real life still goes on in what looks like a museum. You can just hear her muttering about tour groups as she scuttled out of sight.

If you meet a Roxburghe family member on the grounds, they are extremely gracious and truly thankful that "we" are helping them to stay in their home. Can you imagine what it would cost just to have the 365 windows (one for each day of the year) washed? I keep reminding myself of those windows when I pass through the gift shops and tearooms of these glorious old buildings. What a nightmare – I can hardly bring myself to clean one bathroom let alone deal with hundreds of rooms.

The castle grounds are multipurpose and town friendly. You can walk out to the castle or onto the grounds to enjoy the gardens that overlook the River Tweed. The lovely fields are put to economical use with football, agricultural fairs, horse racing, and golf sharing the same site during the year. There are also facilities for walking and picnics.

Kelso Abbey is not much more than the remnants of a once grand ornamental windowed wall but the grace and serenity of the ruin is worth the walk. The old Kelso Bridge just across the street from the Abbey offers a fabulous view of Floors Castle. Way too cute!

Mellerstain House is a short distance north of Kelso and a superb example of a William and Robert Adam design. Building was begun in 1725, and the colors and delicate plaster ceilings of that time are religiously maintained.

Kelso Pottery has a range of stoneware that has been wrapped in straw, oats, barley and reeds and then fired for unusual burnt patterns. They also offer traditional kitchenware with Border landscapes.

Lodging In Kelso

Cross Keys Hotel (36-37 The Square, Kelso TD5 7HL, Ph. 157.322.3303) right on The Square, is definitely in the thick of the action. The weekends might be a little too noisy with wedding parties but if you want evening entertainment, this may be the best bar around. The last time I was there the bar was hoppin' with live music.

Abbey Bank B&B (The Knowes, Kelso TD5 7BH, Ph. 157.322.6550) is a gracious walled house and garden convenient to every part of Kelso. If you have a golfer in tow or you need another country house hotel on your score card, The Roxburghe Hotel and Golf Course (Kelso, TD5 8JZ, Ph. 01573 450331) is the perfect stop. The Duke and Duchess of Roxburghe own this little 200 acre estate and their 18 hole golf course is championship standard. Not a golfer? Then how about attending the shooting school. *Tres Luxe!*

Peebles

I'm not really sure what the specialty of Peebles is. This town has a very "Brigadoonish" feel to it. There are no obvious mills, factories, or farms but there is one long street with lovely shops and galleries. On Saturday morning, the quiet main street fills to overflowing with well-dressed shoppers who linger in lively conversation until the shops close and then, the town is quiet. I don't know where this crowd comes from or how they make their livings but they sure do flock to this place.

The River Tweed meanders behind the shopping street and is buffered from it by a lovely park. You can cross the river on the narrow stone traffic bridge or a romantic footbridge that takes you deeper into the park and on to a nice neighborhood. This is a nice place. Nice isn't bad – nice is nice and you are only 20 miles from Edinburgh. Bus service runs hourly to and from Edinburgh, so this is great day trip destination if a car is not on your agenda.

Peebles Craft Centre is a series of workshops where you will actually see the artists at work. Watch for a sign out on the High Street sidewalk for the Craft Centre which is in Newby Court.

I particularly enjoyed the Dunnydeer Studio Porcelain which features vases that look like grey stones with intricate white lines. You can purchase a series where the white line appears to be continuous as it travels over the pots. Very interesting, and nice jewelry too.

Hilary Forbes Painted Silk was bright with handpainted wares the day I visited, and Bruce Frost was producing some unusual carved and turned wooden pieces at his Woodworks.

The Cornice Museum celebrates the elegant plaster castings that can be seen in country houses, castles and public buildings throughout Scotland. The museum is a plasterer's workshop, unchanged since the turn of the century. Here you'll see how intricate and delicate plaster cornices and ceilings were made and installed.

The oldest inhabited house in Scotland, Traquair House, is just 6 miles from Peebles. Over 800 years ago there were people living here and the family still lives here today. In fact, when Mary Queen of Scots visited in 1566, she had ale brewed on premise, and today the ale brewed here is rated 5 Stars in *Michael Jackson's World Guide to Beer.*

A lively history, which includes intrigue and secret stairs, still plays a major part in the everyday life of Traquair because the main gates to the grounds have been closed since 1745 when Bonnie Prince Charlie passed through them for the last time. You'll come in a side gate just like residents have since that day.

This long history is now being enriched with craft workshops, the High Gallery which supports contemporary painters and needleworkers, antique shops hidden away in the upper reaches of the house and the grounds have a real hedge maze for your enjoyment.

Traquair hosts fairs, festivals and even Shakespeare's plays on the grounds throughout the spring and summer.

Lodging In Peebles

If you walk from town across the footbridge and across the park, you'll come to a very welcoming little hotel that I very much enjoyed. <u>Kingsmuir Hotel's</u> (Springhill Road, Peebles EH45 9EP, Ph. 172.172.0151) resident border collie may have swayed me but even so, the location and my room was lovely.

I like staying in castles but my budget can only stand the princely prices once or twice a trip. Usually I have to settle for a drink in the bar. But Peebles has a newly refurbished castle that is well within the budget. <u>Castle Venlaw Hotel</u> (Edinburgh road, Peebles EH45 8QG, Ph. 172.172.0384) has a turret, other castle necessities and a 4 star rating but not the price usually accorded to castles. It still isn't B&B priced but it is a castle.

<u>Minniebank Guest House</u>, (Greenside, Peebles EH45 8JA, Ph. 172.172.2093) owned by Ken and Brenda Bowie, serves up a view of the Tweed with their bed and breakfasts. This house will fit the budget.

<u>Cringletie House Hotel</u> (By Peebles, Peeblesshire EH45 8PL, Ph. 172.173.0244) looks like a Scottish castle should look, so I'll call it a castle. If prices judge a castle

then this is truly a castle. The award-winning restaurant is a major draw and there must be a fabulous drink to be had in the bar. Splurge on!

I've spent a lot of time talking about a town that often doesn't rate a mention in guidebooks. Why? I guess I could see myself living there. It's nice.

Border's Diversions~

Scottish Borders Council, S.B.C., Arts Development Unit, Library Headquarters, St. Mary's Mill, Selkirk, TD7 5EW.

Freedom of the Fairways, Admail 2193, Jedburgh TD8 6ZY, Ph. 870.607050, or book on-line at www.scot-borders.co.uk.

Hawick Diversions —

Hours & Directions

Jean's, Mrs. Jean Marsden, 4 Wilton Hill, Hawick. On the A7. Retirement was in Jean's plans but the shop, I'm sure, will live on.

Hawick Cashmere Company, Trinity Mills, Duke Street, Hawick. Open year round Mon-Fri during factory hours 10am-5pm. You'll find their sister store in

Edinburgh's Haymarket area but you won't find the same prices.

Peter Scott, 11 Buccleuch St, Hawick. The shop is modern and bright but located in an area of old, sooty mills so you get a very Victorian feeling. It is always amazing that something as gorgeous as Scotland's famous woollens could have made their reputation in such dingy surroundings.

Peter Scott's sweaters can be found at Nordstrom's here in Seattle but once again not at the mill price.

Valeri Louthan at Wiltonburn Country Cashmeres, Wiltonburn Farm. Ph. 145.037.2414. Not a name we commonly recognize here in the U.S., these gorgeous creations are mainly sold in London's finest shops and on the Continent.

Pringle of Scotland, Factory Shop, Victoria Mill, Victoria Road, Hawick. Open year round Mon-Fri 9:30am-4:30pm, Sat 9:30am-1pm during the summer months.

Wright's of Trowmill, Trowmill on the road to Kelso. If your budget or nerves can't cope with cashmere, then the lambswool and Shetland sweaters here will make your heart sing. Great prices and great styles.

Hermitage Castle, 15 miles south of Hawick on the B6399. Open April-Sept, Daily 9:30am-6:30pm. Fee $. Small gift shop only.

Milnholm Cross, 1 Mile south of Newcastleton on the B6357. The cross is right beside the road and access is at all times. Free.

Border Fine Arts Gallery, Townfoot, Langholm. Open year round Mon-Fri 9am-5pm, Sat 10am-4pm.

Lochcarron of Scotland and Cashmere Wool Centre, Waverly Mill, Hudderfield Street, Galashiels. Next to Safeway. Mill shop open year round Mon-Sat 9am-5pm, Sun noon-5pm. Free. Mill tours and museum open June-Sept. Fee $

Melrose Diversions —

Hours & Directions

Melrose Abbey, Abbey Street on the Main Square, Melrose. Open April-Sept daily 9:30am-6:30pm; Oct-Mar daily Mon-Sat 9:30am-4:30pm, Sun 2pm-4:30pm. Fee $.

Abbotsford House, On the B7060 between Galashiels and Melrose. Open Mar-Oct, Mon-Sat 10am-5pm; June-Sept Sundays 10am-5pm; Mar-May and Oct Sundays 2pm-5pm. Fee $$.

Scott's View, on the B6356. 4 miles east of Melrose. Open at all times. Fantabulous view but not at its best in driving rain, cottony fog, or swirling snow.

The Eildon Walk, leave Melrose by the Lilliesleaf Road (B 6359) and watch for the signposted walk. Sturdy shoes are recommended. 1 1/4 hours roundtrip.

Dryburgh Abbey, Dryburgh, St. Boswells, Melrose. On the B6404, 5 miles southwest of Melrose. Open daily 9:30am-6:30pm. Fee $. Small shop and picnic area.

Priorwood Gardens, Melrose, adjacent to Melrose Abbey. Open Apr-Sept, Mon-Sat 10am-5:30pm, Sun 1:30pm-5:30pm; Oct-Christmas, Mon-Sat 10am-4pm, Sun 1:30pm-4pm. Fee $. Shop, demonstration area, and historic orchard picnic area.

Teddy Melrose, The Wynd, Buccleuch Street, Melrose. Open year round 10am-5pm. Tea Garden open June-Oct.

Trimontium Exhibition, Melrose Market Square. Open Apr-Oct, 10:30am-4:30pm. Fee $. Guided Tours on Thurs 1:20pm-5pm. The tour Fee ($) includes tea.

Kelso Diversions –

Hours & Directions

Floors Castle, Kelso. Open daily mid Apr-Oct, 10am-4:30pm. Fee $$. Coffee Shop and Licensed Restaurant. Scheduled events on the grounds most Sundays in summer.

Kelso Abbey, Bridge Street, Kelso. Open at all times. Free.

Mellerstain House, Gordon, Berwickshire. 7 miles northwest of Kelso. Open Mid Apr-Sept, Sun-Fri 12:30pm-5pm. Restaurant open 11:30am-5:30pm. House closed Saturday (I suppose the Earl of Haddington deserves his home to himself for one day). Fee $$.

Kelso Pottery, The Knowes, Kelso. Behind the Abbey. Open year round, Mon-Sat 10am-1pm and 2pm-5pm.

Peebles Diversions –

Hours & Directions

Peebles Craft Centre is located in Newby Court. Look for the sign post and sidewalk sandwich board halfway along the High Street. Hours of shops and studios vary.

Dunnydeer Studio Porcelain, 9 Newby Court, Peebles. Open year round Mon-Sat 10:30am-5pm. Sunday by appointment.

Hilary Forbes Painted Silk, Unit 2, School Brae, Peebles. Open year round Mon-Sat 11am-5pm; June-Sept Sundays 2pm-5pm.

Woodworks, 8 Newby Court, Peebles. Year round Mon-Sat 10am- 5pm.

The Cornice Museum of Ornamental Plasterwork, Innerleithen Road, Peebles. Directly across the street from the Park Hotel. Open year round Mon-Thur 10:30am-12pm and 2pm-5:30pm. Closed weekends and holidays. Donation. Some items are for sale.

Traquair House, Traquair House, Innerleithen, Peebleshire. 6 miles southeast of Peebles on the B709. Open April-Oct daily 12:30pm-5:30pm; June-Aug 10:30am-5:30pm. Fee $$$. Ale tasting every Friday 3-4pm in the Malt Loft. The 1745 Cottage Restaurant is located in the Old Walled Garden. Nice web site at traquair.co.uk.

-13-

Ten Days Without A Car

If you are a true "widow" you may be sick to death of the car. You probably spend more time in the driver's seat than on your own sofa. Kids to lessons and games, groceries, bags of mulch, trips to the dump because "he's golfing", and the endless commute all make you dread a vacation that involves a car. You keep asking yourself "How much can I see and do without a car?" Well...

Scotland may just be the most perfect place to travel without a car.

The train system, linked to a nationwide bus system and small regional bus companies, can get you really out into the countryside. In fact, by taking a leisurely train journey, linked with a regional bus, connecting to a sea going ferry, you could find yourself in front of a peat fire in the Shetland Islands. Now that is really getting away from it for a few days. Many of us would be perfectly content staying in one place, unpacking and taking day trips on the train or bus.

You can do it! And here are the keys:

ScotRail, Ph. 845.748.4950,www.scotrail.co.uk.

Scottish Citylink Bus Company, Ph.870.550.5050, www.cityling.co.uk.

Strathclyde Passenger Transport (SPT), Ph.141.332.7133 a consortium of transport companies serving Glasgow and Ayrshire.

First Edinburgh Bus Co., Ph.131.663.9233, www.firstedinburgh.co.uk. Serves regions adjacent to Edinburgh including Stirling, The Borders and Glasgow.

Caledonian MacBrayne Steamship Co., Ph. 147.565.0100, www.calmac.co.uk.

P&O Scottish Ferries, Ph. 122.457.2615, www.poscottishferries.co.uk.

You can contact these folks directly or ask the Tourist Board for schedules and fares. Each company offers great deals from Cheap Day Return fares to extended travel plans very similar to the Eurail Pass. If you are over 55, traveling in the winter, or interested in exploring the Highlands, then there may be a special for you. Don't be shy, ask questions and be specific about your needs.

Now let's get traveling!

The major international airport of Scotland is just outside of Glasgow but there is also an international airport in Edinburgh. If I had my druthers, I'd fly into Edinburgh and sink directly into a jet lagged reverie of glorious, romantic and historic scenery.

Day 1 - Edinburgh

The airport shuttle bus will deposit you at Waverley Station where you will find a large and efficient Scottish Tourist Board office. If you did not take my advice and pre-book your first night's room, then try to find lodgings that will suit your budget and style. Aim to be as close to the center of Edinburgh as possible. If you are feeling energetic, put your luggage in a locker or "Left Luggage" at the station, wash your face, and start your stay with a city bus tour to get the lay of the land without expending a lot of energy. You can pick up these tours on Waverly Bridge just outside of Waverly Station, right off of Princes Street. Make sure the tour makes stops at the major tourist attractions – Edinburgh Castle, Holyrood Palace and St. Gile's Cathedral. This crash course in Edinburgh 101 will take you to what you should see, and if you find something you really want to go back and explore more thoroughly, then it can be done quickly.

I did one of these tours 30 plus years ago and I put my Mom and Dad on one of these tours a few years back. They raved about how informative the guide was and how nice it was not to have to fumble with guidebooks. They met a nice couple to have lunch with later in the day, and my Dad did go back, early one morning, to St. Giles Cathedral for an extended photo shoot.

After the tour, you will feel the dreaded jetlag closing in, but do not give in to it. The tour will have dropped you back at the Waverly Bridge, and you can pop into the Tourist Office in Waverly Centre and peruse the brochures and flyers. Depending on how you feel, you might like to book a play or musical event for the evening or, maybe wiser, something for your second night. Then you could browse a bit, have a nice meal with lots of fluids, pick up your luggage and find your way to your lodging. Get yourself settled, have a long hot bath, turn on the telly and call it a day. The longer you can stay up, the better you will sleep and morning will see you starting to come around to Scottish time.

Day 2 - Edinburgh

Eat a hearty breakfast because Day Two's list of things-to-do in Edinburgh is endless. Breakfast is a great time to jot down in a small notebook a few things that are near one another so you won't be backtracking. If you aren't interested in art museums, don't put them on your list. Don't waste your time seeing something Cousin Madge would love to see.

Day 3 - Edinburgh & Vicinity

On your third day you'll feel rarin' to go. Here are some ideas to consider: Take a day trip out to Stirling either by train or bus and see another great castle and a very old town, prowl around the narrow wynds and make sure you have extra film. Take a bus out into the Border Region for some excellent woollen shopping at true woollen mills. Take an evening train or bus back to Edinburgh and find some entertainment, stay up late and pack your bags because tomorrow morning there is a train to catch to Glasgow.

Day 4 - Glasgow

On your fourth morning lug your bags to the front hall where your landlady will watch them until you are ready to make the Glasgow trip. The train runs all day long, about every 40 minutes, for an hour trip into the heart of Glasgow. You can do your last minute shopping in Edinburgh, pick your departure time, collect your bags and catch the train. A cab will get you to the station in fine time.

Glasgow's Queen Street Station is right in the thick of the downtown action. You'll emerge onto George Square, one block off of the Buchanan Street Pedestrian Shopping Precinct. You may spy the Copthorne Hotel (George Square, Glasgow G2 1DS, Ph. 141.332.6711, Fax 141.332.4264. This is not a place for just a drink (the bar is open only to hotel guests) but if your budget can't stand the severe jolt of a night at the Copthorne, then I hope you've done a little more homework and found a budget pleaser. Remember my warning about rooms being scarce in Glasgow and book early.

The tourist office is right across George Square for help with "what's on".

Day 5 - Glasgow

On Day 5 you might prowl the museums and shops, ride the underground all day for £2.50 (about $4.50) and book concert/theatre tickets.

Day 6 - Glasgow & Vicinity
Or . . . On To Inverness

On Day 6 take a day trip out to Burns Country, New Lanark Village or a cruise on the River Clyde.

Another option is to pack your bags and take a morning train for Inverness. Stop in Pitlochry for lunch and a poke around town, or take a short tour out to Blair Atholl. You can rejoin the train at 5:30pm, see some spectacular mountain scenery and be in Inverness at 7:15. Find your hotel and hit the streets. This far north, it is light in the summer months until about 10pm so you can enjoy walking in the evening. This may be the stop you find a "Scottish Night" and let loose your best rendition of *Scotland The Brave* or *Oh Danny Boy*.

Day 7 - Inverness

Day 7 is not one of rest. If you chose to arrive in Inverness this morning, you'll have to get crackin'. Find the Victorian Market and look in all the little shops, even the ones up dark rickety stairs, take a cruise on Loch Ness, tour Ft.George on the North Sea, visit the Moor of Culloden and its impressive battlefield and the nearby town of Nairn, or you can look at wallpaper in the D.I.Y. store. Busy, busy, busy.

Day 8 - Aberdeen or St. Andrews

Now it gets tricky. You have two days left before you have to be back in Edinburgh for your flight home on Day 10. I think I'd choose either Aberdeen or St. Andrews not both.

Option 1 - Aberdeen

If you get a move on and catch the 8:42am train to Aberdeen, you'll be there by 11am. The train station is a 15-20 minute walk to all the major sights of the town and if you are going farther a field, then buses are handy here as well.

Contact the Scottish Tourist Board about companies that run tours out to the "Trails". If you want a full plate of Stately Homes, Castles and Distilleries, then this is your best bet.

A lively, international city, Aberdeen, with an active nightlife, beachfront leisure/recreation centers, two universities and several world class museums can keep you more than occupied day and night.

Option 2 – St. Andrews

The same 8:42am from Inverness will drop you at Leuchars where a convenient bus will be waiting to take you into St. Andrews' center. You'll arrive in the early afternoon, have time to put your bags down and still see most of this small university town before dark.

Ancient buildings, bookshops, bistros and coffeehouses are all part of the fun here. Check to see if there is any activity of interest at the university for the evening or climb the tower of St. Andrews Cathedral to see the sunset.

Go to the Tourist Board, right on the main shopping street, for bus or tour information to Crail, a sweet little whitewashed fishing port.

Day 9 - Back To Edinburgh

Look at the train schedule for a mid-afternoon trip into Edinburgh. Check the airport shuttle schedule at the Waverly Station Tourist Board. Get to your hotel. Drop your bags and head out for last minute shopping and a beer to cry in. If you need a box and tape, get it now so you can pack miscellaneous treasures to be checked onto your flight as luggage. Cry in a beer. Take a long glance at The Castle and go home and change for dinner. Have a blow-out because it's your last night. Stagger home and pack.

Day 10 - The Airport

WAAAAAA! Check in. See what is available before you cross the security lines. Sometimes there are great restaurants and shops in the general waiting area so families can spend more time together before the traveler crosses through security. Visit Duty Free for your new found favorite single malt and check for "special value" quick gifts, or maybe a Rolex or two (just kidding!). Have a drink, buy a magazine or calendar, mail your last postcards and try to contain your sobs.

EPILOGUE

The worst part of writing this book and particularly Chapter 13 – Ten Days Without A Car has been the lack of space. I would have loved to have told you about pizza in Inverness, the millions of daffodils in Fraserburgh or how soft a Highland cow's nose is. And then I could have told you about the dress shop in Oban with the terrific sale, or the whimsical pottery pigs in Peebles....

No, this is your trip and you will see many of the things I've seen, and you will find the craziest or most beautiful or tastiest that I've never found. And that is what **your** trip is all about. Have fabulous fun!

And now for some unfinished business...

Appendix

The Golf Widow's Selected Scottish Golf Courses

The Venerable and Foible Laden

There are hundreds of golf courses in Scotland and in Aberdeenshire they are seemingly next door to one another. Choosing the courses to include here was not an easy task, but I tried to choose the premier course of each region and then I went for spectacular scenery, location and finally, odd.

The Scottish Tourist Board can supply you with regional brochures touting courses and special programs available for extended play at budget pleasing prices.

If you are bent on playing golf in Scotland or trying to make a golfer happy, my best advice is to make advance reservations. My dear friend, Alistair, who lives in The Borders, will get on the phone and talk to the course registrar at the club just down the road to make sure he gets his tee time. Golf is a very serious pursuit in Scotland and to be denied can bring one's blood to a boil.

I've included addresses and phone numbers for all of the courses and fax numbers if they are available. Also included are simple directions and some of the peculiar foibles of the individual clubs.

Because most of the clubs require prior arrangements for play, I have not included pricing. When you make contact you will be able to get the current price for a round.

And just one more reminder... Dress is conservative and dressier than in the US. Slacks and a sweater or windbreaker are the norm. Baseball caps are frowned upon, jeans are seldom seen, and pastels... well... they really shouldn't be seen in the US either. If you need a style guideline then watch the British matches on TV. I would steer clear of the tweed knickers, but hey, if your golfer wears pastel plaid, then this may be a sign of his peacock proclivities.

AYR BELLEISLE, Belleisle Park, Doonfoot Road, Doonfoot, Ayr KA7 4DU, Ph. 129.244.1314, Fax 129.244.2632. Follow the signs to Burns Cottage and then onto the A719.

18-hole parkland course next door to Ayr Seafield. Visitors welcome with advanced arrangement. Limited clubhouse facilities.

AYR SEAFIELD, Belleisle Park, Doonfoot Road, Doonfoot, Ayr KA7 4DU, Ph 129.244.1258, Fax 129.244.2632. 1.5 miles south of Ayr on the A719 following signs for Burns Cottage.

18-hole parkland and seaside course next door to Ayr Belleisle. Visitors welcome. Limited clubhouse facilites.

BRORA, 43 Golf Road, Brora, Sutherland, KW9 6QS, Ph. 140.862.1417, Fax 140.862.2157. On the A9 north of Inverness; turn right over the bridge in the center of Brora.

A links course with 18-holes and a practice range. Visitors are welcome and there are clubhouse facilities.

BRAEMAR, Cluniebank Rd., Braemar, Aberdeenshire, AB35 5XX, Ph.133.974.1618. Signposted from the village center, turn left opposite the Fife Arms Hotel.

18-holes of parkland. Visitors are welcome at all times. Full clubhouse facilities.

CARNEGIE CLUB, Skibo Castle, Dornoch, Sutherland, IV25 3RQ, Ph. 186.289.4600, Fax 186.289.4601. Take the A9 north from Inverness and make the first left after Dornoch Bridge. The road will be signposted Meikle Ferry North, go 1 mile and turn right at Green Sheds. If the *Today Show*'s Matt Laurer could find it, then you can too.

Visitors are welcome here on weekdays only. Prior arrangements are necessary. Tee times are restricted to between 11am and 12:00pm. Hold onto your pocketbook for the greens fee is somewhere in the range of $200 for 18-holes, but if you are with a group you can get your 18-holes with soup, sandwiches, and housewine for that same fee. Inquire about this when you book.

CARNOUSTIE, Links Parade, Carnoustie, Angus, DD7 7PH, Ph.124.185.3789. Fax 124.185.2720. 12 miles east of Dundee on the A930.

There are three 18-hole courses here and visitors are welcome by prior arrangement. There are weekend restrictions. This is a British Open host course. Full clubhouse facilities.

CRAIGMILLAR PARK, 1 Observatory Rd. Edinburgh EH9 3HG, Ph. 131.667.2499. Right in town.

18-hole parkland course with full clubhouse facilities. Visitors welcome Wed. and Sun. after 2pm by prior arrangement. Yow! At the time of writing the fees were dirt cheap so I'm sure you need to reserve early.

CRAIL GOLFING SOCIETY, Balcomie Clubhouse, Fifeness, Crail,KY10 3XN, Ph. 133.345.0686, Fax 133.345.0416. Eleven miles southeast of St. Andrews on the A917.

36-holes. Visitors are welcome. They have opened a new 18 hole course, Craighead, so if you can't get on at Crail inquire about that course. Full restaurant service with a view over the North Sea.

CRIEFF, Perth Road, Crieff, Perthshire, PH7 3LR, Ph. 176.465.2397, Fax 176.465.5096. Course is on the A85 on the east edge of Crieff.

27-hole, reasonably priced, parkland "ferntower" course. Visitors are welcome and there are full clubhouse facilities.

EYEMOUTH, The Clubhouse, Gunsgreenhill, Eyemouth TD14 5SF, Ph. 189.075.0551. On the A1107, 1 mile off the A1 near Burmouth.

18-hole seaside course. Visitors welcome any day. Full clubhouse facilities.

FORT WILLIAM, North Road, Torlundy, Inverness-shire, PH33 6SN. Ph. 139.770.4464, Fax 139.770.4464. 2 miles north of Ft. William on the A82.

Visitors are welcome at all times. Bar snacks are available.

FRASERBURGH, Philnorth, Fraserburgh, Aberdeen-shire, AB43 8TL, Ph. 134.651.6616, e-mail fburghgolg@aol.com. South of the first roundabout when entering Fraserburgh and then first right.

27-hole links course. Visitors are welcome. There are bar and dining facilities available.

GLASGOW GOLF CLUB, Killermont, Bearsden, Glasgow, G61 2TW, Ph. 141.942.1713, Fax 141.942.0770. 6 miles northwest of Glasgow near the Killermont Bridge.

18-hole parkland course. Visitors are welcomed by prior arrangement. Lunches and high teas by arrangement so I assume there is no proper restaurant.

GOLSPIE, Ferry Road, Golspie, Sutherland KW10 6ST, Ph. 140.863.3266, Fax 140.863.3393. On the A9 to Golspie.

Visitors are welcome. Bar and catering facilities.

GLENEAGLES, Gleneagles Hotel, Auchterarder, Perthshire, PH2 1NF, Ph. 176.466.2231, Fax 176.466.2134. Halfway between Perth and Stirling on the A9.

Three (count'em) 18-hole, moorland courses. Kings, Queens and the Monarchs courses are open to visitors with reduced rates for hotel residents. Rates start from £75 (about $110) for weekday rounds. Full service bars, grill, restaurant, conference center, spa, and expanses of lush lawn.

HAWICK/VERTISH HILL, Vertish Hill, Hawick, Roxburgh TD9 0NY, Ph. 145.037.2293. Just south of Hawick on the A7.

18-hole parkland course. Visitors welcome with some restrictions on Saturdays and no play before 10:30am Sunday morning. There are full clubhouse facilities during the summer months.

KINGUSSIE, Gynack Road, Kingussie, Inverness-shire PH21 1LR, Ph 154.066.1600, Fax 154.066.2066. Off the A9 and turn in to the club at the Duke of Gordon Hotel.

18-holes on a scenic hilly course. Visitors welcome. Clubhouse facilities.

LOCHCARRON, East End, Lochcarron, IV 54, Ph. 152.072.2229. Drive through the village and keep an eye out. May be best to stop at the Rockvilla Hotel for specific directions as sheep used as signposts are often unreliable.

9-hole parkland and links course. Visitors are welcomed, after the shock wears off of seeing a visitor. I'm not sure why, but the hours of 2pm-5pm are off limits for visitors. Maybe they move the sheep across the course or the shepherds have the prime afternoon hours.

There are no clubhouse facilities but catering can be arranged at the Rockvilla Hotel in the village.

MACHRIHANISH, Machrihanish, Campbeltown, Argyll PA28 6PT, Ph 158.681.0213. Fax 158.681.0221. 5 miles west of Campbeltown on the B843.

18-hole natural links course. Visitors welcome with prior arrangement. Full clubhouse facilities. They also offer accommodation packages.

MALLAIG – TRAIGH GOLF COURSE, Traigh, Arisaig, by Mallaig, Arisaig, PH39 4NT, Ph. 168.745.0337. On the A830 between Ft. William and Mallaig.

9-hole links course. Visitors are welcome and there are snacks available in the clubhouse.

MUIRFIELD (Honourable Company of Edinburgh Golfers),
Muirfield, Gullane, East Lothian EH31 2EG, Ph.162.084.2123.
Course is on the A198 notheast of Gullane.

18-hole links course founded in 1744. Fourteen British Opens have been held here since 1892. I suppose the British Open Governors decided that the course just wasn't up to snuff during the first 140 years of its existence.

To play here you, as a visitor, will be welcomed only on Tues. and Thurs. with prior arrangements. There is full catering and bar service. Ladies, don't forget that you cannot lunch in the clubhouse.

NAIRN, Seabank Road, Nairn, IV12 4HB, Ph 166.745.3208, Fax 166.745.6328. Off the A96 at Nairn Old Parish church.
    18-hole seaside course with a practice range. The 1990 Walker Cup was held here. Visitors welcome by prior arrangement. Full service clubhouse.

NAIRN DUNBAR, Lochloy Road, Nairn, IV12 5AE, Ph. 166.745.2741, Fax 166.745.6897. 1/2 mile east of Nairn on the A96.
    18-hole links course with full club house facilities. Visitors are welcome but because of the most reasonable price, reservations are imperative.

PAISLEY, Braehead, Pailsey, PA2 8TZ, Ph. 141.884.2292, Fax 141.884.3903. Off the M8 at Junction 27 to Braehead.
    18-hole moorland course. Visitors welcome before 4pm. Full clubhouse facilities available.

PETERHEAD, Craigewan Links, Peterhead, Aberdeenshire AB42 1LT, Ph. 177.947.2149, Fax 177.948.0725. On A92 and the A975.

18-hole seaside links course. Visitors welcome with some Saturday restrictions. Full facility clubhouse.

PITLOCHRY, Golf Course Road, Pitlochry, Perthshire PH16 5QY, Ph. 179.647.2792. From the A9 turn onto Atholl Road, then Larchwood Rd to Golf Course road.

18-hole hill course. Visitors are welcomed by prior arrangements with the Pro. Full clubhouse facilities.

POLLOCK, 90 Barrhead Road, Glasgow, G43 1BG, Ph. 141.632.1080, Fax 141.649.1398. Four miles south of City off the M77.

An 18hole, wooded, parkland course open to visitors on weekdays only with prior reservations. No ladies.

POWFOOT, Cummertrees, Annan, DG12 5QE, Ph.146.170.0276, Fax 146. 170.0276. Off the A75 to Annan until signs for Cummertrees and Powfoot on the B724. 3 miles on the B724 make a sharp left after the railway bridge.

18-hole links course. Full clubhouse facilities. Visitors welcome except Sat. and after 2pm on Sun.

PORTPATRICK/DUNSKEY, Golf Course Rd., Portpatrick, Stranraer, DG9 8TB, Ph. 177.6 81.0273, Fax

177.681.0811. Follow the A77 or A75 to Stranraer and follow signs for Portpatrick, then turn right at the War Memorial.

18-hole cliff top links course. Full clubhouse facilities. Visitors are welcome with their handicap certificates.

PRESTONFIELD, 6 Priestfield Road North, Edinburgh EH16 5HS, Ph. 1.667.9665. Near Commonwealth Games Pool.

18-hole parkland course. Visitors welcomed with prior arrangement.

PRESTWICK, 2 Links Road, Prestwick, Ayrshire KA9 1QG, Ph. 129.247.7404, Fax 129.247.7255. One mile from Prestwick Airport and adjacent to the Prestwick Train Station.

18-holes. A host course for the British Open. Visitors are welcome by arrangement. There are full clubhouse facilities but the dining room is for men only.

ROYAL ABERDEEN GOLF CLUB (BALGOWNIE),

Balgownie, Bridge of Don, Aberdeenshire AB23 8AT, Ph. 122 470 2571. 2 miles north of Aberdeen on the A92.

18-hole seaside links. Visitors welcome on all weekdays but restricted on weekends. Full clubhouse facilities.

ROYAL TROON, Craigend Road, Troon, Ayrshire, KA10 6EP, Ph. 129.231.1555, Fax 129.231.8204. 3 miles from A77 and Prestwick Airport.

18-hole links course and one of the British Open host courses. Visitors welcome Mon, Tue, and Thurs only with handicap restrictions. Full bar and restaurant. A budget buster at about $180 a round.

ST. ANDREWS OLD COURSE (founded 1400) and ST. ANDREWS NEW COURSE (founded 1895), St. Andrews Links Management Committee, Pilmour Cottage, St Andrews, Fife, KY16 9JA, Ph. 133.446.6666, Fax 133.447.7036. 60 miles north of Edinburgh on the A91. Train service to Leuchars from the north and the south. The courses are right in the town.

These courses and the 3 others overseen by the Management Committee are very busy. Most welcome visitors but be advised, if you want to play the Old Course you must book very early.

ST. BOSWELLS, Braeheads, St. Boswells, Melrose, Roxburghshire TD6 0 DE, Ph. 183.582.3527. Off the A68 in St. Boswells.

9-holes of just plain cute parkland. Visitors are welcome by prior arrangements. Bar and light snacks are available at the weekend.

TAIN, Chapel Road, Tain, Ross-shire IV19 1PA, Ph 186.289.2314. 35 miles north of Inverness on the A9.

18-hole links course. Visitors welcome. Full clubhouse facilities.

THE ROXBURGHE, Heiton, Kelso, Roxburghshire TD5 8JZ, Ph. 157.345.0330, Fax 157.345.0611. On the A698 between Jedburgh and Kelso.

A new (1997), 18-hole parkland/woodland course. Visitors welcome by prior arrangement. There is a practice range and short game area. The Roxburghe Hotel is on site and offers full facilites and a golf theme bar – Spikes.

TURNBERRY, Turnberry Hotel, Turnberry, Ayrshire KA26 9LT, Ph. 165.533.1000, Fax 165.533.1706. On the A77 15 miles southwest of Ayr.

Two 18-hole seaside links – Ailsa and Arran. Host course for the British Open. Prior arrangements are essential to avoid disappointment. A splurge at about $125 a round. Full service, fabulous clubhouse and hotel.